T0328596

Cambridge Elements ≡

Elements in Metaphysics
edited by
Tuomas E. Tahko
University of Bristol

FORMAL ONTOLOGY

Jani Hakkarainen
Tampere University
Markku Keinänen
Tampere University

Shaftesbury Road, Cambridge CB2 8EA, United Kingdom

One Liberty Plaza, 20th Floor, New York, NY 10006, USA

477 Williamstown Road, Port Melbourne, VIC 3207, Australia

314–321, 3rd Floor, Plot 3, Splendor Forum, Jasola District Centre,
New Delhi – 110025, India

103 Penang Road, #05–06/07, Visioncrest Commercial, Singapore 238467

Cambridge University Press is part of Cambridge University Press & Assessment,
a department of the University of Cambridge.

We share the University's mission to contribute to society through the pursuit of
education, learning and research at the highest international levels of excellence.

www.cambridge.org
Information on this title: www.cambridge.org/9781009069069

DOI: 10.1017/9781009070126

First published 2023

A catalogue record for this publication is available from the British Library

ISBN 978-1-009-06906-9 Paperback
ISSN 2633-9862 (online)
ISSN 2633-9854 (print)

Formal Ontology

Elements in Metaphysics

DOI: 10.1017/9781009070126
First published online: September 2023

Jani Hakkarainen
Tampere University

Markku Keinänen
Tampere University

Author for correspondence: Jani Hakkarainen, jani.hakkarainen@tuni.fi

Abstract: Formal ontology as a main branch of metaphysics investigates categories of being. In the formal ontological approach to metaphysics, these ontological categories are analysed by ontological forms. This analysis, which the Element illustrates by some category systems, provides a tool to assess the clarity, exactness and intelligibility of different category systems or formal ontologies. It discusses critically different accounts of ontological form in the literature. Of ontological form, the authors propose a character-neutral relational account. In this metatheory, ontological forms of entities are their standings in internal relations whose holding is neutral on the character of their relata. These relations are "formal ontological relations". The Element concludes by showing that our metatheory is useful for understanding categorial fundamentality/non-fundamentality, different formal ontologies, and for unifying metaphysical questions. This title is also available as Open Access on Cambridge Core.

Keywords: formal ontology, ontology, metaphysics, metametaphysics, ontological categories

ISBNs: 9781009069069 (PB), 9781009070126 (OC)
ISSNs: 2633-9862 (online), 2633-9854 (print)

Contents

1 Introduction: Against Fantology

Consider two competing world views in a rough outline. According to the first, everything that is consists in a plurality of constantly evolving *processes* in which nothing stays the same. A paradigmatic example of such an entity is a river that is in constant flux. The second presents a completely different view of the fundamental nature of being: it is constituted by *substances*, that is, persisting independent countable property-bearers like inanimate bodies. These world views give different answers to the question about the categories of being. The ultimate metaphysical questions are then what are the *categories of being* (ontological categories, henceforth 'categories', for short) and what are their relations?

Formal ontology is initially the *branch* of metaphysics, a field of study addressing these classic questions. Therefore, an answer to them is *a* formal ontology: a *category theory*. Formal ontology is also an *approach* to metaphysics that provides theoretical tools to discuss the equally perennial methodological follow-up question: how are we supposed to solve the aforementioned problem about categories, including the possible fundamental categories? 'Formal ontology' is then an expression that needs to be disambiguated. It has three different connected meanings: (1) a branch of metaphysics; (2) a category theory; and (3) an approach to metaphysics.

This is primarily an Element about formal ontology as an approach, although we also discuss some contemporary formal ontologies as category theories. Indeed, it is the first systematic, detailed, and historically informed overview of formal ontology. We shall introduce and defend a *second order*, that is, *metatheory* of the formal ontological approach rather than any category theory or an exhaustive overview of contemporary formal ontologies. This metatheory involves an account of formal ontology as a main branch of metaphysics and a nominalist second-order view in which categories – whatever they are – are not entities numerically distinct from their members. The present Element is then primarily an exercise in *metametaphysics* that is, the field of philosophy studying the nature of metaphysics: its subject matter, branches, method, concepts, epistemology, and semantics.

In the formal ontological approach, categories are *analyzed* by the ways in which entities are, that is, by *forms of being* or *ontological forms*, such as being independently. Therefore, ontological forms determine the membership of categories. For example, if an entity exists in an ontologically independent, numerically identical, persisting, and property-bearing way, some formal ontologies as category theories consider it a member of the category of substances. Consequently, a tenable metatheory of formal ontology needs a satisfactory account of ontological form and its difference from being or existence. We will propose such an account later.

Formal ontologists then do not leave categories implicit or intuitive, consider them just part of 'ideology' (Quine 1953: ch. VII),[1] or read categories from the alleged logical form of propositions. By contrast, in the current analytic metaphysics, a general approach directly inspired by the syntax of *predicate logic* has taken a dominant role in formulating the problem about the actual categories and their relations, other metaphysical questions, and competing answers to them. Following the formal ontologists Barry Smith (2005), E. J. Lowe (2013), and Ingvar Johansson (2016), we call it *fantology*. Smith characterizes fantology as:

> [t]he doctrine to the effect that one can arrive at a correct ontology by paying attention to certain superficial (syntactic) features of first-order predicate logic ... More specifically, fantology is a doctrine to the effect that the key to the ontological structure of reality is captured syntactically in the 'Fa' (or, in more sophisticated versions, in the 'Rab') of first-order logic, where 'F' stands for what is general in reality and 'a' for what is individual. Hence, 'fantology'. (Smith 2005: 153–4)

Rather than seeing fantology as any specific category *theory*, we consider it a *paradigm* to conduct metaphysical investigation and the study of categories based on a certain set of unquestioned assumptions. These assumptions can be divided into two larger sub-claims. The first is that there is such a thing as the *logical form* of descriptive sentences spelled out by the well-formed formulas of predicate logic. Consequently, there is a preferred – although perhaps not a unique – way to formulate our descriptions by formalizing them in predicate logic. Second, this logical structure *mirrors* the categorial structure of being. In other words, there is an indirect way to provide an account of the categorial structure by considering how the referring expressions are categorized in predicate logic.

There is a certain family of different views about the categorial structure one can adopt in this paradigm. These views are constrained by taking logical syntax as a model in forming logically correctly structured claims about reality. Similarly, different metaphysical problems and views are formulated by means of the privileged logical language of predicate logic. Finally, the core of the fantological conception is the following *assumption* about *category distinctions*: existents are divided into particulars (the referents of singular terms), on the one hand, and properties and relations (with some definite adicity, that is, the number of places, the referents of predicate terms), on the other.

---

[1] The ideology of a theory consists of predicates only applying to certain entities rather than signalling any commitment to entities corresponding the predicates. By contrast, the ontology of a theory is formed by its commitments to existing things: its ontological commitments. Quinean ideology does not make any sharp distinction between categorial and non-categorial predicates (e.g., *being a substance* vs *being round*).

One popular representative of this approach is the traditional Russellian ontological view that maintains that properties and relations are specific kinds of entities of their own, property or relation universals that are directly possessed (exemplified) by particulars. Here, properties are considered a special case of relations, one-place relations (Russell 1903, 1912, 1918; Armstrong 1978, 1997; Hochberg 2000).[2] Particulars, in turn, exemplify universals with certain specific adicity, that is, the number of 'places'. Thus, the ways properties and relations occur as constituents of reality are constrained by rules completely analogous to those of the logical syntax: like predicate expressions, properties and relations are monadic, dyadic, triadic, and so on, depending on the number of particulars they must be combined with to constitute complete property/relation exemplifications ('facts').

The different *fact ontologies* (e.g., Russell 1918; Armstrong 1978, 1997; Hochberg 2000) develop these ideas further by reifying the exemplifications of properties/relations as facts. Irrespective of one's willingness to assume facts – or any singular entities corresponding to exemplifications of properties/relations – one may assume that *all* basic constituents of reality are possible referents of singular terms or one- or many-place predicates. In first-order predicate logic, one can take an arbitrary open formula 'ϕx' of a given language having only the variable 'x' as free and consider 'ϕx' a predicate expression. According to the *abundant conception of properties*, any such predicate refers to a general entity, 'the property ϕ of x' or 'the property of being ϕ' (the abundant conception is easily generalized to many-place predicates and the corresponding relations). For example, *being a human and that 2+2=4* may be considered a property of David Armstrong in this conception if 2+2=4 is a necessary truth. Hence, predicate expressions are assumed to stand for abundant properties/relations. Similarly, all singular terms are assumed to refer to entities belonging to a single category: *particulars*.

It is important to acknowledge that for drawing the particular/universal distinction, the advocate of the fantological approach must make essential use of *exemplification*: property/relation universals are entities that can be exemplified by (one or more) particulars, but not vice versa. Moreover, they may add that universals are potential referents of predicate expressions ('properties') and capable of multiple location (as wholes, at a time), while particulars are not.[3]

---

[2] Russell was a full-blown advocate of the two central claims of fantology in 'The Philosophy of Logical Atomism' (Russell 1918). In his other works cited here, the general picture is more complicated. We are grateful to the Russell scholar Dr Anssi Korhonen for drawing our attention to this.

[3] See MacBride (2005) for a criticism of the different proposed ways to draw the particular/universal distinction in the fantological context (see also our discussion of this distinction in Section 4).

Thus, a logical syntax-driven generality is characteristic of this fantological conception of particulars, properties, and relations. Properties and relations are referents or denotations of predicate expressions. Properties such as the property of *being red* are 'unsaturated' entities, or rather, worldly counterparts of open formulas ('Rx').[4] Correspondingly, the standard referents of singular terms, particulars are assumed to be *concrete objects*.[5] Particulars have (exemplify, instantiate) properties and are related in different ways. The fantological framework does not specify the categorial nature of 'concrete objects' in any more detail. This seems to have motivated the idea of considering objects *bare particulars*, objects that lack all necessary features except particularity, individuality, and the capability of exemplifying universals.[6]

Within the fantological paradigm, it is in its more recent developments considered the least problematic assumption of an ontological theory that there are particulars.[7] Moreover, concrete objects like stones, humans, and electrons are regarded as the paradigmatic examples of particulars. The main disagreements among the metaphysicians working in this paradigm have concerned the existence and ontological status of properties and relations. One alternative here is to maintain that all entities are particulars (in the sense of concrete objects) and that the predicate terms have a plural reference: they apply to a plurality of particulars.[8] Another, less radical and more popular alternative is to re-construe properties and relations as non-spatiotemporal (i.e., abstract) particulars and individuals: sets of concrete objects (Lewis 1983, 1986).

Since our main purposes in this Element are metametaphysical, our aim is not to spell out the specific difficulties coming with the different metaphysical views formulated in the fantological paradigm (see Smith 2005, Lowe 2013). Instead, let us take another look at the two main sub-claims or pillars of fantology that were mentioned earlier. Both sub-claims were explicit elements of Bertrand Russell's (1918) logical atomism. It seems that they have been

---

[4] Here 'unsaturated' means an entity (property or relation) that must be completed by a certain number of objects in order to occur as a constituent of reality.

[5] In special cases, universals or abstract objects might also be taken as referents of singular terms. In such cases, the special use of singular terms is annotated by calling them 'abstract singular terms' (e.g., see Loux 1978).

[6] Fact ontologists Gustav Bergmann (1967) and David Armstrong (1997) have been prominent advocates of bare particulars, Armstrong calling them 'thin particulars'. See Perovic (2017) for an overview of the recent discussion.

[7] For instance, Armstrong (1978) frames the problem of universals as a question of whether there are properties/relations in addition to concrete particulars (referents of singular terms). Thus, the existence of particulars is considered the least problematic. See also Devitt (1980) and Lewis (1983) for a similar view about concrete particulars.

[8] See Goodman and Quine (1947) for a classical statement of the rejection of other entities than just concrete particulars.

transformed into more implicit background assumptions of a large part of the later analytic metaphysics. One significant transitory figure here was Willard van Orman Quine (1948), who took predicate logic ('canonical notation') as a vehicle for expressing ontological commitments of the different ontological views. Under the influence of Quine and David Lewis (1983, 1986), Quine's criterion of ontological commitment has become a widely – but not unanimously – accepted standard to assess ontological commitments of the different metaphysical views.

Perhaps the mainstream view in Quinean metaphysics has been the reconstrual of properties/relations as sets of particulars. However, the talk about particulars (as referents of singular terms) and properties and relations (as referents of one- and many-place predicates) has still been in a central place in analytic metaphysics and its applications. Moreover, influential analytic metaphysicians (e.g., Armstrong 1978; Loux 1978; Lewis 1986) have taken predicate logical expressions having the form 'Pa' or 'Rab', and so on, or their variants formed in colloquial language such as 'a is P', as a principal tool to formulate metaphysical problems such as the problem of universals[9] and the problem of intrinsic change (see Lewis 1986, 202ff.).

Thus, although there is perhaps not any explicit commitment to the claim about the logical form of all meaningful descriptive sentences, the more recent advocates of the fantological approach have continued the practice of construing descriptive sentences in the canonical notation of predicate logic. Among philosophers working in the paradigm, there has also been disagreement about the existence or nature of certain ontological problems like the problem of universals.[10] These larger-scale disagreements or specific metaphysical disagreements notwithstanding, the advocates of the fantological approach proceed to postulate entities belonging to general categories (particulars, sets, properties, n-place relations, states of affairs) that are put to a one-one correspondence with the categories of the non-logical expressions of predicate logic (see earlier).

Predicate logical language has a structure stipulated by the rules of logical syntax, which tell us how we can form sentences and other well-formed

---

[9] See Armstrong's (1978: 1–17) discussion of the problem of universals and the different (extreme) nominalist answers to that problem. Although Armstrong formulates the problem of universals in terms of common nature in the introduction of the book (Armstrong 1978: xii), he provides the more explicit formulations of the problem by means of properties expressed by the corresponding predicates. In framing the problem of universals, Michael Loux (1978) speaks about 'attribute agreement': he takes it to be an agreed fact that objects have monadic or many-place attributes and suggests that this must be accounted for.

[10] See Lewis' (1983: 201) comments on Michael Devitt's (1980) and Armstrong's (1980) views about the one over many problem ('the problem of universals').

formulas from basic expressions. The fantological approach assumes without any clear argument that this structure could function as a guide to categories. Since we could have constructed a very different kind of formal language, this point of departure seems metaphysically arbitrary. Here serious metaphysical argumentation is replaced with stipulation based on the structural characteristics of *one* artificial language.

Moreover, as Smith (2005: sec. 19) argues, we can apply predicate logic to metaphysical reasoning without making fantological assumptions. The basic strategy is simple. First, we may assume that singular terms are the only expressions referring to specific entities. By contrast, predicate expressions do not correspond to any entities. Rather, we use predicates to make claims about a certain specific type of internal relations, that is, 'formal ontological relations' ('FORs', for short) between entities (see Smith & Grenon 2004; Lowe 2006: ch. 3; see also Section 3).[11] Existential dependence is a good candidate for an FOR. For example, it seems that you depend for your existence on your brain specifically. Then there holds the FOR of specific or rigid existential dependence between you and your brain. The term 'formal ontological relation' comes from the point that they determine ontological forms, by which categories are analyzed. Therefore, we can use singular terms to refer to entities belonging to several distinct categories, described by predicates, such as sets, substances, universals, modes, tropes,[12] processes, and events.

This approach has of course its limitations because it is usually presupposed that singular terms refer to countable entities with definite identity conditions (countable individuals) and it is controversial whether there are fundamentally such entities.[13] In any case, it would be a mistake to assume that there *must be* entities belonging to the single category of 'concrete objects/particulars' corresponding to singular terms because of one's preferred logic.

Looking at things from a different angle, by construing alternative formal languages, we can raise serious doubts against the idea of *the* logical form of our

---

[11] Tentatively, internal relations and hence FORs are relatedness of entities rather than beings numerically distinct from their relata (see later). In general, relatednesses of entities are their standings in a relation to something without reifying this relation as an additional entity. For example, you and this Element stand in the relation of numerical distinctness without there being a third entity: the relation of numerical distinctness.

[12] Tropes are simple or thin particular natures, for example, determinate masses and electric charges (see Hakkarainen 2018; Keinänen, Keskinen, & Hakkarainen 2019). In contrast to modes, which are particular properties of objects, tropes do not primitively modify or characterize their bearers (Lowe 2006: 97).

[13] Johanna Seibt (2018) introduces the monocategorial ontology of general processes, which are not countable as discrete units. Similarly, Lowe (1998: ch. 3) argues that not all entities need to be considered 'countable individuals'.

descriptions being revealed by their translation to a language constructed in accordance with the rules of logical syntax of standard predicate logic. For instance, philosophers of language and metaphysicians (e.g., Gupta 1980 and Lowe 2009) have developed logics for common names/sortal terms, which are not considered specific kinds of predicates.[14] These developments are significant in showing that we need not rely solely on predicate logic in an exact description of metaphysical problems such as the problem of universals.

Formal ontology as a branch of metaphysics is the investigation of ontological forms and categories. They are studied directly in it, without recourse to the peculiar characteristics of a representative medium, for instance, predicate logic. Categories are analyzed by ontological forms rather than read from the categories of representations. Ontological forms provide a tool to assess the clarity, exactness, and intelligibility of different category systems or their parts. Fantology, by contrast, constitutes a misleading attempt to construct a basis for formal ontology as a category theory by means of a single representative medium. Fantology is a theoretical straitjacket that makes it hard to see alternative category systems that do not easily fit it, such as certain process ontologies and trope theory. We will argue that the formal ontological approach liberates metaphysics from the fantological straitjacket.

This we can learn by beginning from a different starting point than in fantology: metaphysics and ontology in the phenomenological tradition. Accordingly, we will summarize Edmund Husserl's (1859–1938) and his students Edith Stein's (1891–1942) and Roman Ingarden's (1893–1970) metaviews of formal ontology in the next section. It leads us to Smith's, Kevin Mulligan's, and Peter Simons' introduction of formal ontology to analytic metaphysics from phenomenology in Section 3, which also includes discussing Lowe's (1950–2014) formal ontology and strong essentialism. In Section 3, we will argue further that neither Smith, Simons, nor Lowe has advanced a tenable account of ontological form. We shall defend our alternative character-neutral relational theory of ontological form in Section 4. It builds the foundation for our nominalist relationalism about categories in the same section. Section 5 is devoted to corroborating our metatheory of ontological forms and categories by showing what we can do by it. In this final section, we apply our theory to the fundamentality and non-fundamentality of categories, the analysis of some category theories, such as priority monism and trope theory, and the unification of metaphysics, its branches, and problems.

---

[14] Moreover, Lesniewski's Ontology is a logical system that has expressive power comparable to first-order predicate logic, but whose non-logical expressions can all be considered as individual or plural names (see Simons 1982).

2 A Very Short History of Formal Ontology

2.1 Edmund Husserl

'Formal ontology' is a technical term introduced by Husserl in his *Logical Investigations* (1900–1) (Husserl 1970, vol. 1: 310).[15] To understand formal ontology, which is our present aim, we need then to take a quick look at Husserl's notion of it. His notion is connected to the intentionality of consciousness that was one issue that drove him in his way up to *Logical Investigations* (Richard 2015; Moran 2017). Intentionality was a central topic to his teacher Franz Brentano (1838–1917) (*locus classicus*: Brentano 1973: 68). Intentionality and understanding it properly are, indeed, essential to his phenomenological approach (Moran & Cohen 2012: 167).[16] Every conscious act like perceiving intends towards something (*etwas* in German), be it a tree or triangle (Moran & Cohen 2012: 170).

Husserl is then motivated to describe formal ontology repeatedly as considering something in general (*etwas überhaupt*) or object as such (*Objekt an sich*). Object as such is any possible thing (*Ding*) whatsoever that can be the bearer of predicates true of it (Moran & Cohen 2012: 228, 317). Indeed, in Husserl's theory of judgement, object is anything of which something is predicated; one may predicate green of the tree, for instance (Moran & Cohen 2012: 174–5). Since the notion of this kind of object is very thin in content, it comes close to possible entity or being and should not be understood as a concrete or abstract particular, not to speak of Kant's thing in itself. Yet an object as such should be something *that really can exist*, that is, a possible object, such as a concrete particular like a tree (Hartimo 2019). Ontology as a science of essences[17] and hence formal ontology must concern possible objects in Husserl's view. Therefore, formal mathematics cannot offer us a formal ontology. It does not concern what really can exist; it is too far-removed from perception for that (Hartimo 2019).[18]

Nonetheless, what offers us a formal ontological theory is one thing, what formal ontology as a field of study is, is another; we need to distinguish a theory representing a formal ontology from a theory or view *about* formal ontology as

---

[15] This section is written for our systematic purposes and is not therefore intended to be an exercise in Husserl, Stein, or Ingarden scholarship, still less in phenomenology.

[16] As it is to Alexius Meinong's (1853–1920) theory of objects (*Gegenstandstheorie*), which distinguishes the psychological content of experience from intentional object (Marek 2021).

[17] Husserl believes that we can intuitively grasp the pure essence or *eidos* of any object by varying its features freely in imagination and discerning what stays the same throughout the variation process. Pure essence thus refers to the invariant features or necessary form without which the investigated phenomenon is inconceivable (Belt 2021; cf. Spinelli 2021).

[18] According to Hartimo (2019), Husserl realised this as late as 1929 in *Formal and Transcendental Logic* (Husserl 1969).

a field of study. Taking the latter *meta* perspective, which is the main business of the present Element, we can say that Husserl's meta view of formal ontology is that it is *an a priori formally universal science of possible objects as such and their categories*. Its *formality* consists initially in the point that objects and their categories are abstracted from anything *material*, that is, specific concerning them (Hartimo 2019). In terms of this distinction between form and matter, the determinate hypotenuse of a specific right triangle is an example of a part materially speaking, but what it is to be a part in general is a formal issue. Accordingly, Husserl's examples of the categories of possible objects as such, that is, formal categories include part, whole, object, relation, property, state of affairs, magnitude, oneness, and identity (Moran & Cohen 2012: 26; see Husserl 1982: §10). The formal *universality* of this science consists in its unrestricted applicability to anything whatsoever that really can exist, to what Husserl calls 'any object-provinces whatever' (Husserl 1969: 120). For example, what it is to be a part is supposed to apply to any domain of possible objects; any such domain includes parts.

Thus, Husserl characterizes the notion of the *form of object* by universal applicability in the 'provinces' or 'regions' of possible objects as such (Husserl 1969: 120). Forms of objects are such that their notions are applicable to every region, that is, domain of possible objects as such investigated by ontology. Therefore, we may use the notion of *ontological form* instead of form of object, even though Husserl does not. According to him, ontological forms are neutral on the domains of possible objects as such. Parts as an example of ontological forms are to be found in principle in any domain of possible objects as such. Ontological forms are *domain neutral* in Husserl.

By the distinction between objects as such formally and materially speaking, Husserl divides ontology into formal and material or regional ontology (Moran & Cohen 2012: 49; Smith 1989: sec. 5). Formal ontology studies the ontological forms and categories of possible objects as such. Its domain is universal, whereas any material ontology has a more restricted but still very general domain distinguished by their matter as contrasted with ontological form (Moran & Cohen 2012: 278). For example, geometry investigates the domain of ideal spatial beings and biology investigates the domain of living beings (Moran & Cohen 2012: 278). Husserl's notion of material or regional ontology has affinities with the German early modern philosopher Christian Wolff's (1679–1754) notion of *special metaphysics* since Husserl thinks that even such very general domains as mind and matter have corresponding material or regional ontologies (Moran & Cohen 2012: 277–8). According to Wolff, for example, rational psychology is a special metaphysics investigating the essence of the soul (Wolff 1963: 35; see Section 5.3.3 for further details).

Husserl's view that formal ontology studies formal categories connects him to a significant but not so generally well-known historical background issue: an Aristotle renaissance in the nineteenth-century German-speaking world (Albertazzi 2006: 43; Hartung, King, & Rapp 2019: 2–4). Its manifestations were the critical editions of Aristotle and many philological and philosophical commentaries (Hartung, King, & Rapp 2019: 2–4). Partly due to Kant's and Hegel's influence, a central issue in it was how to make sense of Aristotle's view of categories and whether his list of them in *Categories* can be derived from something or at least justified *contra* Kant's well-known criticism of Aristotle in this respect (Albertazzi 2006: 53–4). A key figure in the renaissance was Husserl's teacher at Vienna, Brentano, who was taught by an earlier giant of the movement, Adolf Trendelenburg (1802–72) in Berlin. Aristotle is one of the essential sources of Brentano's philosophy, whether we are speaking about cognition, logic, or morals (Albertazzi 2006: 59).

Nowhere is this truer than in metaphysics. It started already in Brentano's dissertation of 1862 on the several senses (*Bedeutung* in German) of being in Aristotle (Brentano 1975), which was an outstanding contribution to the literature on Aristotle's categories. Those that are there share the *state* sense of 'being' (*Sein*). Your friend and you, for instance, share the state of being since you are there. It differs from the *thing* sense of 'being' (*Seindes*), which covers being*s* (things) and their totality (everything). Brentano's chief argument is that Aristotle's list of categories can be justified, correspond to the real divisions of the totality of being, and provide an ontological unification for the different state senses of being (Simons 1992: 383–4; Albertazzi 2006: 54–6). The state sense of being of (primary) substance is the focal point to which every other state sense of being like that of qualities and quantities is connected (Simons 1992: 384; Politis 2004: 103ff.). Brentano also reduces the number of Aristotle's categories from ten to eight (Albertazzi 2006: 57).

The details of all this do not matter so much for the present purposes. The main point is that without claiming direct influence from Brentano's dissertation to Husserl on formal ontology, the issue of categories both in Aristotle and in general was a much-discussed topic in Husserl's immediate philosophical context. Accordingly, it makes sense to read Husserl on formal ontology from this perspective. Formal ontology in Husserl already is linked to the Aristotelian metaphysical tradition in which categories are central (see Alfieri 2015: 92; Ingarden 2016: 71). He himself relates formal ontology to Aristotle explicitly in *Formal and Transcendental Logic* (Husserl 1969: 80), where he criticizes Aristotle of lacking it but does not elaborate on the connection between Aristotelianism and formal ontology.

2.2 Edith Stein and Roman Ingarden

One of Husserl's best pupils, Edith Stein, did more of this elaboration after her conversion to Catholicism in 1922 and subsequent intense studies of Aquinas.[19] In 1931, Stein composed a manuscript, revised later in 1935, entitled *Potency and Act: Studies toward a Philosophy of Being*, which was published posthumously in German in 1998 (Stein 2009).[20] In its second part (*Act and Potency from the Perspective of Formal Ontology*), Stein develops her own account of the notion of ontological form, its difference from ontological matter, and hence her view of formal ontology as a branch of ontology.[21] Although its origin is in Husserl, Stein's view differs from her teacher's account (Alfieri 2015: 103).

Stein's view is that the notion of fullness (*Fülle* in German) distinguishes ontological form from ontological matter. One of her analogies is a geometrical shape, say, a ball, and the stuff that is ball-shaped. When we abstract the stuff ('fullness') from the ball, its shape, that is, a geometrical form is what remains (Stein 2009: 27). Stein says that an individual being (*Einzelsein*), a physical object like the ball, is concrete in the sense of being qualitatively and quantitatively full: a determination of qualities like colour and shape and quantities such as mass and volume (Stein 2009: 28). When we consider emptying it of this fullness completely, we have its ontological forms: something (*aliquid* in Latin) or object (*Gegenstand*), what it is (*quod quid est*) and being or existence (*Sein*). These three are the basic ontological forms, which are empty of qualitative and quantitative fullness (Stein 2009: 28).

Accordingly, Stein characterizes ontological matter as qualitative and quantitative fullness, whereas ontological form is what is left when this fullness is emptied. Ontological form is always fulfilled by ontological matter as there is no being without fullness and every ontological matter occurs in a form (Stein 2009: 28). It is ontological form that is studied in formal ontology, while material ontology investigates beings in their fullness and existents in their

---

[19] Stein was a holocaust victim and Catholic martyr (canonised in 1998) who entered a Carmelite monastery in Cologne in 1933. Her religious name is Saint Teresa Benedicta of the Cross.

[20] *Potency and Act* and other ontological works by Stein may be seen as a part of new ontology that evolved in Germany in the 1920s after the heyday of neo-Kantianism: for example, Hedwig Conrad-Martius (1888–1966), Nicolai Hartmann (1882–1950), Max Scheler (1874–1928), and Martin Heidegger (1889–1976) (Peterson 2019: xvii). In his *Ontology: Laying the Foundations* (*Zur Grundlegung der Ontologie*, 1935), Hartmann (2019: 3) also mentions Meinong's theory of objects in this context even though it was developed before the First World War when neo-Kantianism still dominated philosophy in Germany. However, Meinong was born and spent his professional career in the Austrian empire where neo-Kantianism did not have the same position (Damböck 2020: 173).

[21] Stein (2009: 69) might have been the first to use the term 'ontological form' ('*ontologische Form*' in German).

different genera (Alfieri 2015: 96). A formal ontology is the 'theory of the forms of being and of beings' (Stein 2009: 27).[22]

Near the end of the first part of *Potency and Act*, Stein argues that any description or saying in any area of beings presupposes ontology and formal ontology (Stein 2009: 25). This makes sense regarding metaphysical descriptions and sayings since her view of ontology as distinguished from metaphysics is Husserlian. The domain of ontology consists of the essences of any possible objects as such, and metaphysics is the study of what is. Metaphysics then presupposes ontology and formal ontology.

Stein as a formal ontologist is still understudied. Therefore, together with Husserl, the most influential phenomenologist for formal ontology in contemporary metaphysics and metametaphysics, which we will discuss in the next section, is the Pole Roman Ingarden. He studied first with Kazimierz Twardowski (1866–1938), who was a student of Brentano, in Lwów (now Lviv in Ukraine), and then under Husserl's guidance in Germany. Ingarden disagreed with Husserl when he thought that Husserl turned to transcendental idealism from realism in *Ideas Pertaining to a Pure Phenomenology and to a Phenomenological Philosophy – First Book* (1913; Husserl 1982). Ingarden was apparently so taken by this turn that his magnum opus considers how to put the distinction between idealism and realism precisely: the three-volume *Controversy over the Existence of the World* (2013, 2016, the two first volumes), originally published in Polish in 1947–8 (the two first volumes) and in German in 1964, 1965, and 1974 (the third volume posthumously).

Ingarden's great work includes the most extensive metadiscussion of formal ontology as a branch of ontology to date. In line with Husserl and Stein, Ingarden considers ontology the a priori discipline of what is essential to possible objects in general (Simons 2005a: 40–1). Ontology differs from metaphysics that investigates what is: for example, whether there are properties. Ingarden divides ontology into *existential*, *formal*, and *material ontology* (hence, the three volumes of the *Controversy* on existential, formal, and material ontology, respectively) (Millière 2016: 68).

Existential ontology studies *existential moments* (*existentiale Momente* in German): aspects of existence. Without going into the details unnecessarily, existential moments include different ontological dependencies and independences: existing dependently and independently in various ways. Existential moments constitute *modes of being* (*Seinsweisen*, *Seinsmodi*). Ingarden thinks that being in the state sense is literally modified by existential moments rather than unified. One of the modes of being, being ideal, for instance, consists of

---

[22] For a detailed discussion of formal ontology in *Potency and Act*, see Alfieri (2015: 103ff.).

Figure 1 Misu and Pippo

certain existential moments: being ideal is existing in a certain way. Being ideal and being real are modes of being also studied by existential ontology. Modes of being, in turn, constitute *ontological forms and categories*, for instance, substances, properties, relations, and states of affairs. It is these forms and categories that formal ontology investigates by attempting to solve problems like what it is to be a relation, independently from the actual existence of relations (Simons 2005a: 40–1; Chrudzimski 2015: sec. 4; Millière 2016: 68–9).

Ingarden has a highly detailed and intricate discussion of the ontological notion of form in contrast to that of matter in chapter VII of the second volume of the *Controversy*. We can only summarize Ingarden's way of drawing the ontological form/matter distinction here. To illustrate it, let us ponder an everyday case. Consider the length of Pippo the cat (Figure 1, right), which is longer than the length of Misu the cat (Figure 1, left). Suppose that both lengths are tropes in Ingarden's ontological terms: they share the form of what it is to be a trope (see Section 5.2). By contrast, what makes Pippo's length longer than Misu's length is the ontological matters of these two tropes, that is, the determinate lengths with which the tropes are identified. Here we may use Ingarden's primitive (i.e., non-definable) concept of pure qualitativeness in the broadest sense including quantitativeness and qualitativeness in the narrow sense (Ingarden 2016: 29). The ontological matter of tropes universally is their pure qualitativeness. Material ontology, as a branch of ontology, studies the qualitative in this sense. For example, Ingarden would consider the question of why the two tropes are length tropes rather than, say, height tropes a problem primarily in material ontology. Instead, the question why they all are tropes is a formal ontological problem. Being a trope is ultimately constituted by certain existential moments that are aspects of existence and hence ontologically primary. The ontological matter of a trope is its qualitative nature (in the broadest sense), while its form is its way of existence. The latter is then the privation of the pure qualitative that is the former.[23]

Ingarden's conclusion is that form in the ontological sense is 'the radically unqualitative as such, in which stands the qualitative in the broadest sense ["the pure quality as something that fills-out a form"]' (2016: 52; see 23, 44, 67). Form has 'absolute heterogeneity with respect to any "quality"', and it 'can never occur without that whose form it is' (2016: 67, 68). On the one hand, the ontological form of being a trope is independent from whether a trope is a length, height, mass, or possibly anything else. On the other hand, each possible trope is 'filled out' by something purely qualitative, that is, ontological matter. We are not saying that this is very transparent, we only hope to convey the rough idea in Ingarden. In a similar manner as in Stein, ontological form is emptiness of the qualitative in the broadest sense including qualities and quantities: what is left of an entity when everything qualitative is abstracted from it (Ingarden 2016: 26).[24]

We may therefore distil three distinct concepts of ontological form from the phenomenological formal ontological tradition: (1) domain neutrality in terms of the domains of possible objects as such in Husserl; (2) emptiness of qualitative and quantitative fullness in Stein; and (3) Ingarden's radical unqualitativeness as the emptiness of the qualitative in the broadest sense. We will make some systematic observations about these concepts in the subsequent sections.

Although Ingarden distinguishes ontological forms from modes of being, from a bird's-eye view the phenomenological formal ontological tradition may be seen as being connected to the older and wider tradition of modes of being. According to the latter, being in the state sense is literally modified rather than unified. As was seen earlier, in Aristotle, for example, substances are in a different sense than accidents (qualities and quantities); the former are there independently in contrast to the latter being there dependently upon the former (Politis 2004: 108). The modern representatives of the mode of being tradition include Brentano in his dissertation, Ingarden, and Meinong (existence and subsistence (*Bestand* in German) as modes of being; see Marek 2021).

---

[23] Therefore, Ingarden would not say that tropes are qualitatively identical with each other in that they are each tropes; their membership in the category of tropes is not a qualitative matter even in the broadest sense.

[24] Ingarden's account has clear affinities with Stein's view. An influence could be speculated here. Apparently, Ingarden read that part of the manuscript of *Potency and Act* (Stein 2009) that Stein reused in *Finite and Eternal Being*, which was published posthumously in German in 1950 (Ingarden 2016: 71, 78).

Nowadays 'ontological pluralism', or 'pluralism about being', by Kris McDaniel (2017) and Jason Turner (2010), continues this tradition of thought. It does not entail the classic doctrine that modes of being are represented by different copulas or that being is a property. McDaniel (2017) and Turner (2010, 2012) have argued that modes of being 'are most perspicuously represented by different fundamental quantifiers' (Simmons 2022: n. 1). The opposite view that being in the state sense is unitary is 'ontological monism' (Simmons 2022: n. 1).

In principle, ontological form may be considered in such a manner that the form literally modifies being: the ontological form, say, of a trope modifies the being of the trope in contrast to that of its bearer. Therefore, a formal ontology can belong to the mode of being tradition, as in Ingarden. However, as will be seen later, that is not necessary. A formal ontologist can be an ontological monist.

3 Contemporary Formal Ontology

3.1 Formal Ontological Theories

The explicit entrance of the phenomenological idea of ontological form and formal ontology into contemporary metaphysics occurred in Barry Smith's 1978 paper discussing primarily states of affairs. In this paper, Smith's main reference point of formal ontology is reasonably Ingarden (Smith 1978: n. 11). Furthermore, like Ingarden, Smith, together with Kevin Mulligan and Peter Simons, is a fierce defender of realist phenomenology.

Mulligan, Simons, and Smith drew attention to Husserl's treatment of wholes and parts in the third *Logical Investigation* (e.g., Smith & Mulligan 1983). This resulted in the ground-breaking *Parts* by Simons (1987), in which he studies different kinds of *mereological theories* and their applicability to concrete entities introduced in different contexts. Simons also considers modal mereology and different kinds of relations of *ontological dependence* in connection with mereological relations. One of the main outcomes of Simons' discussion is a systematic treatment of modal existential ontological dependence, such as rigid or specific dependence defined partly by a modal concept and existence (Simons 1987: ch. 8). For example, it seems that you depend for your existence on your brain specifically since it appears not to be possible that you exist, and your brain does not exist.

Simons' discussion challenges 'Hume's dictum' that there are no (metaphysically) necessary connections between wholly distinct entities. Whether Hume himself held the dictum or not, it has been widely assumed in analytic metaphysics, especially by the twentieth-century philosophers such as

Armstrong (1983) and Lewis (1986: 87) (see Wilson 2015: 138).[25] In opposition to this, Smith (1981), Smith & Mulligan (1983), and Simons (1987: ch. 8) argue, learning from Husserl's and Ingarden's formal ontology, that it makes sense to speak about necessary connections and hence ontological dependencies between wholly distinct entities. In part as a result of this, there has been a lively discussion on different kinds of ontological dependencies, which has opened new avenues of thinking in metaphysics (see Tahko & Lowe 2020).

Another application of the formal ontological approach to metaphysics is the neo-Aristotelian four-category ontology by Lowe (2006) developed from Aristotle's *Categories*.[26] According to Lowe (2006: 21–3, 110–13), there are four fundamental categories: substances, modes, kinds, and attributes. Any entity is either a substance, mode, kind, or attribute. Substances and modes are particulars, kinds and attributes are universals. The former cannot be instantiated by numerically distinct entities, whereas the latter do possibly have numerically distinct instances (Lowe 2006: 21–3). This is a formal ontological account of the distinction between *universals* and *particulars* that is independent of the veracity of Lowe's four-category ontology. Followers of Russell on universals and contemporary Platonists about them may adopt it by using a subtly different relation from instantiation, such as exemplification or participation. The formal ontological way of drawing the distinction is arguably superior to other ways of making it in the literature (see Section 4.2).

Lowe's four-category system may be illustrated by Pippo the cat, who is a substance instantiating the kind domestic cat (*Felis catus*) (Figure 2). This kind is characterized by the attribute of regurgitating hairballs of fur, for instance.[27] Pippo is, in turn, characterized by the mass mode of four kilograms that instantiates the corresponding determinate mass attribute. He exemplifies the attributes of both regurgitating hairballs of fur and the mass of four kilograms, but these exemplifications are constituted differently in Lowe's view (2006: 40). Pippo exemplifies the attribute of regurgitating hairballs of fur since he instantiates the kind domestic cat that is characterized by this attribute. Pippo is characterized by the mass mode of four kilograms that is an instance of the corresponding mass attribute.

---

[25] For Hume's view of the matter, see Hakkarainen (2012).

[26] Since we discuss only formal ontologists in this section, we omit contemporary category theories and metatheories of categories that do not analyze categories by ontological forms and that are not then formal ontological (e.g., Westerhoff 2005; McDaniel 2017; Paul 2017; Seibt 2018).

[27] We follow Lowe's spelling 'characterization' when we are using his technical term.

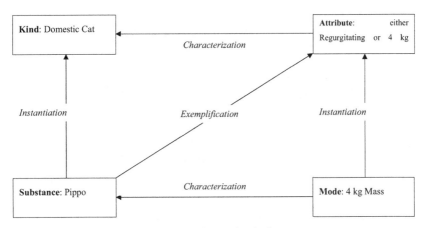

Figure 2 Lowe's ontological square

The mass is something that Pippo has *occurrently*, whereas he has only a *disposition* to regurgitate hairballs of fur; he does not have to do that occurrently or at all. This disposition does not have to be manifested by him. Lowe (2006: 31–2) proposes that one of the major advantages of his category system is that it gives an ingenious explanation for the distinction between occurrent and dispositional predication by way of the two different constitutions of exemplification (see Lowe 2013: ch. 3).[28] The former consists of a substance characterized by a mode instantiating an attribute. The latter is constituted by the substance instantiating a kind characterized by an attribute.

Instantiation, characterization, and exemplification, as well as numerical identity and composition, belong to FORs in Lowe's system (2006: 35). Due to avoiding Bradley's relation regress, FORs are internal relations in the *eliminativist* sense: they are not entities numerically distinct from their relata, like Pippo and the kind cat (Lowe 2006: 44–6, 2012a: 242). Formal ontological relations only hold of their relata (see Keinänen, Keskinen, & Hakkarainen 2019: 521–4). Still, the corresponding relational truths are made true and metaphysically necessitated by the existence of the relata (Lowe 2006: 103).

Another explicitly neo-Aristotelian formal ontologist is Smith. Unlike Lowe, he holds a six-category system in which occurrents form two additional categories to Lowe's four categories. Table 1 is 'The Ontological Sextet' by Smith (2005: 17).

The FORs holding between these categories may be seen in Smith's diagram in Figure 3.

---

[28] For other reasons why Lowe holds realism about universals and his four-category system, such as providing truth-makers for natural law statements and hence a better account for laws of nature than Armstrong and Humeans like Lewis, see Lowe (2015).

Table 1 Smith's ontological sextet

	Independent continuant	Dependent continuant	Occurrent (process)
Universal	Second substance *cat* *ox*	Second quality *headache* *suntan*	Second process *walking* *thinking*
Particular	First substance *this cat* *this ox*	First quality *this headache* *this suntan*	First process *this walking* *this thinking*

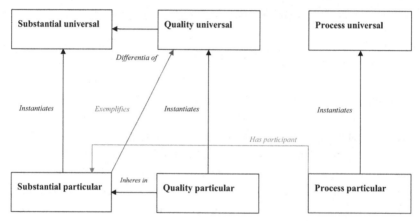

Figure 3 Smith's system (2005: ch. 19)

While Lowe has the same relation of characterization holding between modes/attributes and substances/kinds, Smith has two distinct FORs: inherence and differentia. Inherence is not the same relation as Lowe's characterization since it does not involve identity dependence but specific existential dependence (Arp, Smith, & Spear 2015: 96). In Smith, quality particulars depend for their existence on their specific bearers (substances), whereas Lowe (2006: 27) thinks that modes depend for their identity on substances. Differentia is roughly the good old Aristotelian *differentia specifica* distinguishing a genus into its distinct species (Arp, Smith, & Spear 2015: 69). Accordingly, Smith thinks that quality universals differentiate substantial universals into genus/species structures like animal and rational animal. Furthermore, he proposes that process particulars have participants in substantial particulars. Pippo, a substantial particular, may, for example, participate in the process particular of walking, which instantiates the process universal of walking. Smith thus follows the formal ontological particular/universal distinction. Based on the sextet, he has, together with his colleagues, developed Basic Formal Ontology 2.0, which has dozens of specific applications in medical science (Arp, Smith, & Spear 2015: 160–1). This establishes that formal ontology is also practically useful.

3.2 Ontological Form and Category

The upshot is that formal ontology is a rewarding approach to metaphysics. Nevertheless, its tenability hangs eventually on whether a satisfactory account of the notion of *ontological form* can be given, which we will discuss critically next. Lowe does not give such an account. He only makes remarks about it and its distinction from 'ontological content', which seems close to the notion of ontological matter by the earlier mentioned phenomenologists (Lowe 2006: 48–9). What is clear though is that Lowe thinks that FORs like instantiation define the ontological forms of entities, which is a *relational* view that we will build upon in the next section (Lowe 2012a: 48).[29]

Smith does not really address the notion of ontological form in his first paper on formal ontology (Smith 1978). That happens in his 1981 article (Smith 1981) and especially in a joint 1983 piece with Mulligan (Smith & Mulligan 1983). In these papers, Smith defends an *operational* account of ontological form as well as logical form. According to Smith and Mulligan, one can exhaustively determine the meaning of a logical constant, such as the conjunction sign, by means of purely syntactical operational rules. First, we have formation rules that determine which strings of symbols involving the conjunction sign are syntactical. Then we have transformation rules for manipulating these strings, such as introduction and elimination rules.[30] Similarly, Smith argues, one can determine the meanings of formal ontological terms like 'is an integral whole', 'is a part of', and 'is existentially dependent on' (Smith 1981; Smith & Mulligan 1983). Thus, the test for whether a given feature is formal lies in trying to formulate purely syntactical rules that fully capture the meaning of the term for that feature.

However, Smith has not defended this operational account for decades and probably for a good reason. It is not a very plausible idea that the meaning of formal *ontological* terms could be captured by some purely syntactical rules. One problem here is that there can be a genuine metaphysical disagreement about the principles concerning formal ontological terms like *being a proper*

---

[29] Note that this relationalism does not mean that FORs are entities; Lowe holds an eliminativist view of FORs.

[30] See MacFarlane (2017: sec. 6) for a critical discussion of this inferential characterization of logical constants.

part of and it is not clear which of these principles would be sufficiently indisputable to define their meaning.[31]

Accordingly, characterizing ontological form by *domain neutrality* is the most recent proposal by Smith and Simons, adopted in the 1990s (Smith 1998: 19; Simons 1998: 389; Simons 2009: 144–5, 147; Arp, Smith, & Spear 2015: 31–2).[32] As was seen earlier, it stems from Husserl. Recall that Lowe does not really provide any account of ontological form. Since this is the state of the art, in our critical discussion we will concentrate on the domain neutrality view. Smith is the only one who elaborates on it, and we will target his view in our criticism.

According to Smith, the defining feature of a formal ontological concept is its domain neutrality individually (Arp, Smith, & Spear 2015: 31). Simons does not define domain anywhere, but Basic Formal Ontology 2.0 by Arp, Smith, and Spear does (2015: 32): 'A *domain* is a delineated portion of reality corresponding to a scientific discipline such as cell biology or electron microscopy.' Since no 'matter what science one is considering it studies entities', every scientific discipline has a domain – that is, a delineated portion of entities it studies (Arp, Smith, & Spear 2015: 31). Note that this discipline and hence a domain may be rather specific like cell biology (Arp, Smith, & Spear 2015: 31).

Neutrality is indifference to domain distinctions. Thus, each domain neutral concept or term is individually indifferent to domains. It is applicable across all domains of entities and in all scientific disciplines (Arp, Smith, & Spear 2015: 27). Every formal ontological concept is claimed to be individually domain neutral (Arp, Smith, & Spear 2015: 31). Therefore, all of them apply individually to any domain of entities and 'in all scientific disciplines whatsoever' (Arp, Smith, & Spear 2015: 31). Domain neutrality concerns concepts separately, not their disjunctive pairs or strings, such as 'abstract or concrete'. This is motivated by the point that a formal ontology is supposed to be a 'top-level ontology' that applies to each domain-specific ontology (Arp, Smith, & Spear 2015: 37–8). According to Arp, Smith, and Spear, the most obvious example of a formal ontological concept is the notion of entity, which applies

---

[31] Simons (1987: 362) claims that the principles of minimal mereology lay down '[t]he formal skeleton of the meaning of "part"'. However, even the weak supplementation principle accepted in minimal mereology has been put to dispute (Smith 1987): an object with a proper part, *p*, has another distinct proper part that does not overlap *p*. On the other hand, the advocates of extensional mereologies would accept stronger mereological principles. It is not clear which of these disputes would concern metaphysical views and which are about the meaning of the term of *being a proper part of*.

[32] These authors do not properly argue for the domain neutrality account of ontological form; they just state it.

to anything that exists (Arp, Smith, & Spear 2015: 2, 31). Their other main examples are 'object' and 'process' (Arp, Smith, & Spear 2015: 2, 31).

However, not all plausible examples of formal ontological concepts are individually domain neutral. There are counter-examples to the account. Consider, for example, the notion of proper parthood that is prima facie applicable to many kinds of concrete existents, such as animal bodies and concrete artefacts; they have proper parts. By contrast, if one assumes abstract entities like sets or numbers, they need not be considered as being in any mereological relations to numerically distinct entities. The elements of a set bear the membership relation to the set, but they are not parts of the set. The notion of proper parthood is not applicable to the domain of set theory as a field of mathematics. Thus, even though mereological relations hold between entities belonging to different kinds of domains, there is no need to assume that they are applicable to *all* domains of scientific disciplines. If they are not universally applicable, they are domain dependent or specific rather than domain neutral. But it is difficult to deny that mereological relations in metaphysics are formal ontological. Smith is, indeed, explicitly committed to proper parthood and parthood being formal ontological (Arp, Smith, & Spear 2015: 28, 32).

There are additional plausible counter-examples to the domain neutrality account. According to Smith and Pierre Grenon (Smith & Grenon 2004), different relations of ontological dependence are formal ontological. However, they are not perhaps applicable to the entities belonging to all different kinds of domains. For example, one could construct an ontology, according to which entities in some domain (say, mental beings) are mutually independent simple entities while there is a network of dependence relations among concrete entities. Similarly, it is controversial whether the concept of object is applicable in the domain of fundamental physics (as documented by French 2019), or the concept of process is applicable in the domain of abstract mathematical entities. If object and process are not domain neutral, then, by the domain neutrality account, they are not formal ontological concepts, which would be an unwelcome result for the concepts that are paradigmatic-ally formal ontological by Smith's lights (Arp, Smith, & Spear 2015: 31, 91).

One might respond to this criticism by saying that domain neutrality does not require application in all domains – it suffices that a concept applies in many domains. However, one then faces 'the cut-off point problem' of making a principled clear-cut distinction between categories or formal ontological concepts and natural kinds or natural kind concepts; categories are not natural kinds (Westerhoff 2005: 136). The concept of the electron applies in many domains because it applies in the domains of different sciences. Nevertheless, if this concept 'cuts nature at its joints', it is a natural kind notion rather than a formal ontological concept.

The conclusion is that neither Smith, Simons, nor Lowe has given a satisfactory account of the notion of ontological form, which is something we will provide in the next section. We need such an account to hold the useful formal ontological account of *category*, which is a classic philosophical topic. In the formal ontological approach, categories are analyzed by ontological forms. Lowe thinks that categories are not numerically distinct entities from their members (Lowe 2006: 41–4). He does not identify categories with anything, not even with universals, to avoid regress worries about categories of categories (Lowe 2006: 80, 92, 111, 167). Lowe is not a realist about categories although he is a realist about universals. Among formal ontologists, he clearly differs from Smith who is a realist about both: 'Categories are those universals whose instances are to be found in any domain of reality' (Arp, Smith, & Spear 2015: 31).[33] Rather, Lowe thinks that categories are groups of entities standing in the same FORs as a matter of mind-independent fact (2006: 41–4). Lowe has a *relational* view of categories, as well as of ontological form. Recall that modes, for instance, are entities that characterize substances and instantiate attributes. Take any mode whatsoever and this holds true of it. Therefore, Lowe believes that categorial distinctions are real in the sense of being mind-independent features of the world that we try to understand by formal ontological theories (2006: 43).

Whatever one thinks about Lowe's specific category system, a major advantage of his view of the analysis of ontological forms and categories is that it makes the analysis by FORs systematic and transparent. This increases clarity, exactness, and intelligibility in contrast to the fantological paradigm that leaves categories implicit or considers them intuitively, primitive, or part of the Quinean ideology. One must not confuse kind universals with property universals, for instance. Whether the theoretical virtues of clarity, exactness, and intelligibility are truth-tracking or not, it is difficult to judge an account of a category or an entire category system if one does not know precisely what one is judging. Lowe's view provides a useful metaphysical tool to clarify competing accounts of categories and category systems. This makes it possible to assess them in an exact manner: whether their FORs or ontological forms analyzing categories are acceptable even by a priori consideration, whose justification is independent of experience. According to the formal ontological view about metaphysics, metaphysics is essentially concerned with identifying categories (e.g., Lowe 2018: 14).

---

[33] For other realist views about categories, see Grossmann (1983: 6), Tegtmeier (2011: 178), and Cumpa (2011: 42).

As will be seen later, we can also develop a promising account of what it is to be a fundamental or non-fundamental category based on Lowe's view. At this point, suffice it to note that according to him, the membership of each of the four fundamental categories is analyzed by the standing of entities in the FORs of instantiation and characterization that are *not* constituted by any further such relations (Lowe 2006: 40, 58). Rather, instantiation and characterization constitute ontological dependencies such as rigid existential dependence (Lowe 2006: 37). In themselves, they are unconstituted. Unfortunately, Lowe left the constitution of FORs unexplained, which is an issue we will cover later.

Before Lowe, Simons formulated a view at the turn of the millennium that, borrowing a term from mathematics, 'factors' determine categories (Simons 1998: 381, 389, 2005b: 561). He talks about 'anatomizing' category distinctions by factors instead of considering them brute facts (1998: 382). Like in Lowe, this has the advantage of making category distinctions clear and distinct, unlike in fantology. It is easy to confuse modes and tropes, for instance. Anatomizing these distinct categories by means of factors helps us to keep them apart: modes modify or characterize their bearers, primitively perhaps, while tropes are parts of their bearers and their inherence in their bearers is analyzed by further relations (Hakkarainen 2018). Indeed, Simons (2010, 2012: 137–8; 2018: 41–2) later concluded that the factors are formal and relational: they are mind-independently holding formal ontological internal relations and domain neutral.

Simons and Lowe hold a very similar relational view of categories. Basically, the only difference between them is that Lowe does not adopt the domain neutrality account of ontological form. Earlier, Simons said categories are concepts (1998). Nowadays, he believes that there are no categories numerically distinct from their members but still categorial distinctions are mind-independent (2018: 37). Simons claims that they are '*Aristotelian*' or '*ontic categories*' that are fundamental divisions of mind-independent reality. He distinguishes them from '*Kantian or auxiliary*' categories, such as some logical constants and existence, that do not 'structure reality'. They are only concepts needed for knowledge and understanding (Simons 2018: 40). The concept of existence, for instance, does not structure reality in any manner since it applies to every entity whatsoever. Still, it helps us to understand reality; it is auxiliary.

In Simons' (e.g., 2018: 42, 45–6) view of formal ontology, the influence of Brentano's dissertation, Husserl and especially Ingarden is explicit. As we recall, Ingarden thinks that existential moments (e.g., ontological dependencies and independencies) form modes of beings which constitute, in turn, ontological forms: categories. Simons' disagreement with this is that the distinction between existential moments and modes of being is not needed (2005a: 41). By simplifying Ingarden's account in this respect and by adopting the notion of factor, Simons ends up with his view that relational formal factors or FORs anatomize categories, which is practically the view Lowe holds (Simons 2018: 42).

3.3 Lowe's Strong Essentialism

Simons notes that it is 'perhaps no coincidence that Brentano and Ingarden were regarded by their respective contemporaries as "scholastic", an epithet I also heard used about Jonathan [Lowe]' (2018: 42). There is some truth to that epithet since Lowe is a card-carrying neo-Aristotelian. This is obvious in his four-category ontology, which is very much inspired by Aristotle's *Categories* (e.g., Lowe 2012a). Lowe also says (2012b: 941) that his account of *essence* is 'neo-Aristotelian', or, what is nowadays known as 'non-modal', a term that is familiar from Kit Fine (1994): 'In short, the essence of something, X, is *what X is*, or *what it is to be X*'(Lowe 2018: 16).[34] For example, Pippo's essence is tentatively what Pippo is, or what it is to be Pippo. Lowe believes that particulars have an *individual* essence in addition to the *general* essence of some of their general kinds, including categories (Lowe 2018: 16).[35] By contrast, universals have only general essences. Thus, Pippo has a general essence as an instance of the domestic cat: what it is to be a domestic cat. To be exact, his individual essence involves his general essence as a domestic cat: what it is to be the individual of the kind domestic cat that Pippo is, distinct from any other domestic cat like Misu (Lowe 2018: 16). Therefore, what it is to be Pippo is his individual essence and what it is to be a domestic cat is his '*specific* general essence'. His most specific category, that is, living beings, is his '*fundamental* general essence': what it is to be an entity of that category (Lowe 2018: 17).

A crucial point about Lowe's non-modal account of essence is that to avoid the infinite regress of essences of essences, an essence is not an entity numerically distinct from the entity whose essence it is (Lowe 2018: 20–1). Rather, its essence is expressed by the *real definition* specifying what it is to be, or what it would be to be, that entity, the kind domestic cat for instance, rather than defining a word or concept (Lowe 2012b: 935). Real definition is another classic Aristotelian conception entertained by Lowe (Politis 2004: 299–300; Koslicki 2012: 200).

Lowe's neo-Aristotelian essentialism concerns his view of formal ontology, too. He says in the beginning of the *Four-Category Ontology* that entities divide

---

[34] In contemporary metaphysical literature, there is also a *modal notion of essence*: roughly, the necessary properties of an entity (see Robertson Ishii & Atkins 2020: sec. 1).

[35] 'Individual' versus 'general' essence is traditional terminology. Its use does not mean that Lowe thinks that only particulars are individuals: entities having numerical identity and countability. For a Lowe-inspired essentialist view without individual essences, see Tahko (2022).

into categories in virtue of their intrinsic or non-relational character. His considered view (Lowe 2018: 16), which is also explicitly stated at least once in the *Four-Category Ontology*, is that the intrinsic character is *non-modal essence*: 'that in virtue of which it is the very entity that it is' (2006: 207). He says that 'it is part of the essence of any entity that it belongs to a certain ontological category' (Lowe 2006: 207; see Lowe 2012a: 242–3).

According to Lowe, entities have fundamental general essences that determine their most specific category. In Pippo's case, that is living organisms, which constitutes one of the most specific categories subsumed under the highest category of substances (Lowe 2018: 17). Since non-modal essences are expressed by real definitions, part of the real definition of an entity is its category membership and fundamental general essence. For example, what it is to be a living organism and that he is an organism is Pippo's fundamental general essence that is part of his individual essence and real definition. Consequently, Lowe's considered view is that entities are members of categories and have fundamental general essences in virtue of their non-modal essences (2012a: 242, 2018: 17). Pippo, for instance, belongs to living organisms and has the fundamental general essence of what it is to be a living organism in virtue of his individual non-modal essence. Since ontological forms, that is, FORs analyze category membership in Lowe, he must think that entities have also their ontological forms and stand in FORs because of their non-modal essences, individual (particulars) or general (universals). This is 'serious essentialism' about ontological forms and categories (Lowe 2018: 15–17).

Lowe also holds essentialism in the sense that essence precedes existence ontologically as well as epistemically (2018: 21). Ontologically, this means that 'it is a precondition of something's existing that its essence – along with the essences of other existing things – does not preclude its existence' (Lowe 2018: 21) Epistemically, one can generally know or at least grasp the general essence of something prior to knowing whether anything of that kind exists (Lowe 2018: 21–2; see Lowe 2013: 99, 110, 114). Essentialism in this sense should also concern ontological forms and categories since they are part of the general essence of an entity. The fundamental general essence of an entity determines its most specific category. For example, what it is to be a mode together with the (formal) essences of substances and attributes do not preclude the existence of a mode in Lowe's system, and one can know or at least grasp what it is to be a mode prior to knowing whether modes exist. The ontological form and category of an entity is prior to its existence in Lowe. Lowe holds 'serious essentialism' about ontological forms and categories.

Next, we will show how one can hold a Lowe-inspired relational view of ontological forms and categories without a commitment to Lowe's serious or any non-modal essentialism about them. It is coherent to learn from Lowe and not to endorse his strong modal metaphysics.

4 Our Metatheory of Formal Ontology

4.1 Ontological Form: The Character-Neutral Relational Account

4.1.1 Ontological Form

In the previous section, we concluded that the formal ontological approach to metaphysics hangs on the tenability of the notion of ontological form. We also argued that there are difficult counter-examples to Simons' and Smith's Husserl-influenced account of ontological form as domain neutrality. Next, we will argue that we can formulate a tenable character-neutrality relational account, which has affinities with Ingarden's radical unqualitativeness as such and Stein's proposal of the emptiness of qualitative and quantitative fullness. Tentatively, the ontological form of an entity is its character-neutral relational way of existence. One might think, for instance, that sets exist dependently on each of their elements. Character neutrality is indifference to what entities are like, especially their qualities and quantities, rather than their domains; the existential dependence of a set is indifferent to what its elements are like. A notable consequence of this proposal is that categories are not determined by what entities are like but by the character-neutral relational way of their being. This makes sense since categories are categories of being rather than partitions based on what entities are like (e.g., natural kinds).

To argue for our account of ontological form, let us consider three features of entities typically considered formal ontological, as was seen earlier: *being numerically distinct from*; *being a whole of*; and *being a proper part of*. Each of these is *relational*: they are features that entities have in virtue of being related to something; for instance, one is a whole in virtue of being related to some entities – that is, to one's proper parts, like one's torso. These relational features of entities may also be initially characterized as *ways in which entities exist*: x exists *as* numerically distinct from y, x exists as a whole of y and z, and x exists as a proper part of y. Consequently, these three features may be said to be the *relational ways of existence* of entities – the existence of entities is their standing in a relation to something.

Actually, here we use 'way' in the sense of 'form'; in these examples, we are speaking about the specific *form* of the existence of x. Therefore, we may say that the relational way of existence of x is its *relational form of existence*.

Why is this so, and what are these relations that constitute the relational form of the existence of x?

Let us introduce the concept of *character neutrality* at this point by considering the technical *primitive* (i.e., non-definable) concept of 'character', which is familiar to contemporary metaphysicians and has affinities with Ingarden's notion of quality in the broadest sense.[36] Paradigmatic examples of characters are the qualities (in the narrow sense) and quantities entities presumably have, such as shape and rest mass. One of your characters is, for instance, your rest mass; it is something that you are *like*. Character can then be elucidated as follows: the character of an entity is what the entity is like. As a result, properties are characters. There can also be characters that entities have in virtue of being related to something, that is, relational characters (see Section 4.2.1). In principle, a character may be essential, necessary, or contingent to an entity.[37] Obviously, your rest mass is only contingent to you. Thus, the concept of character here is different from any concept of essence in the sense that while character includes essences, it also covers other characters than essences. Since it covers possible non-modal essences even when they are not considered properties (as in Lowe), the concept of character does not equal with the notion of property either. Hence, we may initially say that character neutrality is indifference to what an entity is like.

Thus, a character-neutral relation holds independent of the character of its relata: it is possible that it holds of the relata even if the character of the relata is different. When its holding is stated, the statement as such, even if true, does not say anything whatsoever about the character of the relata. Therefore, character-neutral relations are such relations whose holding is expressible by true relational statements that do not describe the character of the relata without further assumptions.

Entities with different characters – or perhaps with no character at all – can have the same relational form of existence. For example, we are numerically distinct from smart phones and vice versa although humans and smart phones are very different entities in their characters. Indeed, suppose there are bare particulars, which is an ontological assumption not to be decided by a metametaphysical theory. Then they have the same relational form of existence of numerical distinctness as you have even though, by definition, they do not have any character at all. Thus, we may tentatively conclude that the

---

[36] Contemporary metaphysicians using 'character' or 'nature' in this sense include Armstrong (e.g., 1989: 43), Keith Campbell (1990), some non-modal essentialists (e.g., Fine 1995: 281; Lowe 2018), Douglas Ehring (2011), John Heil (2012: 66) and L. A. Paul (2017: 33ff.).

[37] Whenever we talk about modalities, we speak about metaphysical modalities. Our argument does not rest on any specific account of metaphysical modalities.

relational form of existence is character neutral: entities with different characters or no character at all can have the same relational form of existence.

The aforementioned three relational forms of existence are character neutral. This we can see by considering the *statements* that x is numerically distinct from y, that x is a whole of y and z, and that x is a proper part of y. None of them, *without further assumptions*, describe the character of x, y, and z at all. As such, it does not tell us anything about the character of x, y, and z that x is numerically distinct from y, that x is a whole of y and z, or that x is a proper part of y. They only tell us about the way of existence of x as either numerically distinct, a whole, or proper part. Therefore, these are *formal* statements: they concern the relational form of the existence of their relata.[38] *Ontological form* is then a general concept covering all these three typical examples: standing in certain character-neutral relations. *Being numerically distinct from, being a whole of,* and *being a proper part of* are ontological forms. Other plausible candidates for typical examples of ontological forms include *being a part of* and at least some *types* of *depending ontologically on*, such as *depending for its existence rigidly on* (see Tahko & Lowe 2020).

Let us follow the clue of the three paradigmatic formal ontological examples. Since they are paradigmatic, they generalize: true relational statements about ontological forms do not say anything about the character of entities without further assumptions. Ontological forms of entities consist of or may be construed as their standing in character-neutral relations. Since the order of character-neutral relations might make a difference, the order is to be reckoned. Proper parthood, for instance, is asymmetric (and standardly dyadic). Thus, to be precise, *for an entity to have an ontological form* is *for it to be a relatum of a character-neutral relation or relations jointly in an order.* For you to have the ontological form of, say, a whole is for you to be a terminus of the character-neutral relation of proper parthood; you have proper parts.

As such, ontological form differs from logical form; to a first approximation, ontological form concerns entities, whereas logical form, if there is any, concerns truths or truth-bearers *qua* true or false (see Smith & Mulligan 1983: 73). Thus, logical connectives such as negation and disjunction are not formal ontological, though they might be character neutral. It is a different metaphysical question as to whether there are corresponding formal ontological concepts.

Consequently, the concept of *ontological form* is a complex concept that consists of the concept of *form*, of which we have a character-neutral relational

---

[38] For the grounds of why these forms of existence are not entities in the category of properties, see Section 4.1.4.

account, and the concept of *existence*, which we assume to be univocal and interchangeable with the concept of *being* in the state sense (see Section 4.2.3). For example, for you to have the ontological form of being numerically distinct from something is for you to be the relatum of the character-neutral relation of numerical distinctness from that something. Your distinctness does not modify your being; it is only that you exist *and* stand in the relation of numerical distinctness to something. We hold *ontological monism* about existence and *relationalism* about ontological form.

4.1.2 Generic Identity

The 'is' in 'for you to have . . . is for you to . . .' is 'the is of generic identity': (for an entity) to have an ontological form *is generically identical with* (for it) to be a relatum of a character-neutral relation or relations jointly in an order. Therefore, we need to introduce the notion of *generic identity* next. It will turn out to be beneficial for capturing ontological form, categories, and their typologies in an original manner. Generic identity is a form of *generalized identity*, which is a newcomer notion in philosophy, although its candidates are familiar – for instance, 'for an entity to be a bachelor is for it to be an unmarried adult male' and 'for an entity to be a water molecule is for it to be an H_2O molecule'. Ground-breaking work on generalized identity has been done by Augustin Rayo (2013); Øysten Linnebo (2014), who coined the term; Cian Dorr (2016); Fabrice Correia (2017); and Correia and Alex Skiles (2019).

We follow Correia and Skiles and consider generalized identity analogous to familiar *objectual identity* (e.g., 'Hesperus is Phosphorous'). Logically, Correia and Skiles (2019: 645) express generalized identity 'with an operator, $\equiv$, indexed by zero or more variables, which takes two open or closed sentences and yields another'.[39] A crucial difference between them is that while objectual identity requires that the expressions flanking = *designate* (name) an individual entity, generalized identity does not require this. The truth of generalized identity statements does not hinge upon the relation of designation holding from the expressions flanking $\equiv$ to some entities (Correia & Skiles 2019: 642–3).

Generic identity is a generalized identity of the form 'for an entity to be F is for it to be G' in the monadic case, which can be generalized into polyadic cases that involve relational predicates such as character-neutral relational terms. Generic identity, just like objectual identity, is reflexive, symmetric, and transitive (Dorr 2016: 43; Correia & Skiles 2019: 646, 650). It has transparent linguistic contexts concerning only metaphysical matters, such as formal

---

[39] For the logic of generic identity, see Dorr (2016) and Correia and Skiles (2019).

ontological, rather than their mode of presentation (Dorr 2016: 44; Correia & Skiles 2019: 646). We follow Correia and Skiles (2019: 649) and consider generic identity a primitive concept.

The expressions flanking ≡ can be conjunctive (Correia & Skiles 2019: 644). Yet, Correia and Skiles (2019: 645) emphasize that a generic-identity statement as such does not commit us to the existence of conjunctive properties or facts, which some might find metaphysically problematic. Unlike objectual identity, the relata of generic identity do not have to be entities or the flanking expressions of the sign of generic identity need not be designating, true or satisfied. For example, it may hold for 'for an entity to be a bachelor' and 'for it to be an unmarried adult male', even if there were no bachelors – that is, unmarried adult males. In a word, generic identity is *non-factive*: the truth of the flanking expressions is not a necessary condition for the truth of a generic-identity statement. This is like the truth conditions of equivalence: for example, 'p & (p & ¬p) iff (p & ¬p)' is true, even though neither 'p & (p & ¬p)' nor '(p & ¬p)' is true. That the relata of generic identity do not have to be (designated) entities will turn out to be crucial for our metatheory since we will argue later that character-neutral relations are not entities.

Generic identity allows for *representational* differences between the left-hand side and the right-hand side of ≡ (like the objectual identity, 'Virginia Woolf is Virginia Stephen'). Therefore, representational asymmetry is possible, and the right-hand side may be importantly informative about the left-hand side. Thus, the generic identity of the ontological form of an entity with its standing in character-neutral relations jointly in an order may very well be symmetric *and* informative (Section 4.2.2).

4.1.3 Responses to Possible Objections

Numerical identity and instantiation, exemplification, or participation are further plausible examples of ontological forms. In our construal, they are also relational and character neutral, although some might have reservations about this claim. These reservations might be due to two points:

(1) Numerical identity is usually defined as the equivalence relation satisfying the principle of the indiscernibility of identicals. Therefore, a true statement that x is numerically identical with y says something about the intrinsic characters of x and y, namely, that they are indiscernible.

(2) The realist statements about universals involving instantiation, exemplification, or participation seem to describe the character of at least one relatum of the relation. If it is true that a ball instantiates redness or participates in it – to use a common-sense illustration – then it seems that this true

statement does tell us something about the character of the ball, namely that it is red. A corresponding, nominalist-friendly case can be made of inherence, modification, or characterization (assuming it is formal ontological): if it is true that a red trope or mode modifies, characterizes, or inheres in a ball, then it is true that the ball is red.

We can respond to these worries at the outset.

(1) This possible objection involves the further assumption that x and y have some character or are some characters. A metametaphysical view of ontological form should not rule out the possibility that x and y are numerically identical and do not have any character or are not any characters; entities without any character are trivially indiscernible (e.g., bare particulars or haecceities). Thus, the mere true statement that x is numerically identical with y does not say anything more about x and y without further assumptions about their character.

(2) It is also a further assumption that the property universal that the ball instantiates, exemplifies, or participates in is identified with the character of redness, or any character. The mere statement that the ball instantiates something or participates in it does not really tell us anything about the character of the ball. When we are speaking about instantiation, exemplification, or participation in general metaphysics, we are not primarily speaking of any *token* of this relation but of instantiation, exemplification, or participation as a highly general *type* of relation. In general, the mere statement that x instantiates y or participates in it does not describe the character of x in any way; it only describes x's relational feature of instantiating something or participating in it.[40] For instance, entity y could be a category without any character if categories were formal universals. It is only when we assume something more or less specific about y that x's instantiation of y determines x's character somehow. Instantiation, exemplification, or participation may be understood as a character-neutral relational concept. The corresponding point is correct about inherence, modification, or characterization in nominalism: it is an additional assumption to their holding that the trope or mode is identified with a character, say the thin character red. It is better not confuse, to use Husserl's distinction, formal ontological and material ontological concerns.

---

[40] An objection here is that this statement tells us something about the character of y: it is a universal. Our response is that it does not describe the character of y as a universal because universality is being possibly instantiated; instantiation defines universality rather the other way around. Hence, universality is not a character of y. It is a form of being. We are grateful to Donnchadh O'Conaill for raising this objection to us.

4.1.4 Internality of Character-Neutral Relations

If for an entity to have an ontological form is for it to be a relatum of a character-neutral relation or relations jointly in an order – for instance, numerical distinctness – are these relations internal or external? Next we will argue that these relations are better considered *internal* on the eliminativist account that they are not entities numerically distinct from their relata, in contrast to *external* relations (Hakkarainen & Keinänen 2017: 654; Hakkarainen 2018; see Simons 2012: 137–8).[41] The view that they are external relations leads to a vicious infinite relation regress, which does not ensue for the internal-relation account. These two explanations are exclusive and exhaustive among the relational views of ontological form. Our argument against the external-relation explanation is therefore a *reductio ad absurdum*. By the exclusiveness and exhaustiveness, it is an indirect argument for the internal-relation account and for the view that ontological forms are not additional entities.

Suppose for the sake of our indirect argument that ontological forms are external relations and hence reified as numerically additional entities to their relata. Are these relations universals or particulars? Both realists and nominalists mostly agree on the existence of particulars. Let us therefore suppose further that these relations are particulars. It is also a fairly uncontroversial assumption that there are non-relational particulars (e.g., objects). Hence, we can plausibly suppose nominalism according to which there are both non-relational and relational particulars and only particulars to make the argument simpler. In this nominalist framework,[42] the following infinite regress about the ontological form of numerical distinctness ensues for the reificationist external-relation account for it:

(1) Suppose that there are non-relational and relational particulars and only particulars, which are numerically distinct entities.

(2) Thus, there is an arbitrary particular non-relational entity x [from (1)].

(3) Thus, x is numerically distinct from something [from (1) and (2)].

(4) Suppose that the ontological form of x *being numerically distinct from* is reified as a relational entity between x and something [this is the reificationist external-relation explanation].

---

[41] It is a fairly common view among analytic metaphysicians nowadays that internal relations are not numerically distinct entities, but relations actually holding of entities, expressed by true relational statements (see Armstrong 1978: 86; Campbell 1990: 99–101; Heil 2009: 316–17; 2012: 144–6; Simons 2010: 204–5; 2014: 314–15; Lowe 2012a: 242; Betti 2015: 89; Hakkarainen, Keinänen, & Keskinen 2018; Keinänen, Keskinen, & Hakkarainen 2019). For example, Mulligan (1998), Herbert Hochberg (2013: 232), and Fraser MacBride (2020) disagree on this.

[42] For realist arguments within the framework of the four-category ontology, see Lowe (2006: 80, 92, 111, 167). The last of these arguments can be advanced by assuming only modes or tropes and objects – that is, without assuming universals.

(5) Thus, there is an arbitrary particular relational entity y that is identified with *the numerical distinctness of* x [from (1) to (4)].

(6) If something necessarily true of x is necessarily false of y, then x is not identical with y [the modal version of the non-identity of distinguishables (the contra-positive of Leibniz's Law)].

(7) The ontological forms of being non-relational and being relational are necessary to the entities whose ontological forms they are.

(8) Being non-relational and being relational are exclusive.

(9) Thus, entity y is numerically distinct from x [from (1), (2), and (5) to (7)].

(10) Suppose that the ontological form of y *being numerically distinct from* is reified as a relational entity between y and something.

(11) Thus, there is an arbitrary particular relational entity z that is identified with *the numerical distinctness of* y [from (1), (9), and (10)].

(12) Necessarily, if x is identified with F (e.g., *the numerical distinctness of* y), then x is F.

(13) Thus, entity z is numerically distinct from y and x [from (2), (5), (6), and (11) to (12)], and so on *ad infinitum* (cf. Hakkarainen & Keinänen 2017: 654).

Two explanations about this argument are in order. First, step 9 – that entity y is numerically distinct from x – follows partly from a highly plausible principle. This principle is the modal version of the non-identity of distinguishables. Entities x and y are not identical, because something is necessarily true about x that is necessarily false about y – that x is a non-relational entity. Arguably, the ontological forms of non-relationality and relationality are exclusive and necessary to the entities whose ontological forms they are.

In step 13, the numerical distinctness of z from x follows in this way, too, but for its distinctness from y, we need a further plausible principle (12) that necessarily, if x is identified with F, then x is F. Since y is identified with the numerical distinctness of x, z is identified with the numerical distinctness of y, and it is concluded in step 9 that $x \neq y$, so y and z are numerically distinct by the modal non-identity of distinguishables (6).[43]

Second, we advance this regress argument in the context of explaining the *global* matter of fact that all supposed non-relational particulars are numerically distinct (steps 1 to 3). This fact is represented by the numerical distinctness of an arbitrary non-relational particular whatsoever, that is, x. Here the *explanandum* concerns an ontological form rather than the truth of the statement that the arbitrary non-relational particular x is numerically distinct (step 3) or giving

---

[43] The argument does not presuppose that y, z, and so on are relational tropes. In principle, they may be relational particulars of some other category (e.g., relational modes).

truth conditions for it (accordingly for steps 9 and 13). Therefore, the *explanandum* cannot be accounted for by merely giving truth conditions for the statement that x is numerically distinct. We should underline, however, that the problem that the *explanandum* poses is not an existence question of whether or why there are numerically distinct non-relational particulars. Rather, the problem is globally *formal ontological*: why are all entities of a certain category numerically distinct *given* there are such entities?

From this point of view, one can see that the infinite regress is vicious since it represents an explanatory failure about a global metaphysical problem (see Bliss 2013). The initial task of explanation is to account for a universal matter of fact: the numerical distinctness of all non-relational particulars. The *explanans* is to postulate a relational particular y, which is identified with the numerical distinctness of an arbitrary non-relational particular: x. Therefore, y is also an arbitrary particular of the universal type 'the numerical distinctness of an arbitrary non-relational particular'. The second *explanandum* is the numerical distinctness of y, which is accounted for by the postulation of another relational particular z, identified with the numerical distinctness of y. Again, z is an arbitrary particular of the universal type 'the numerical distinctness of the arbitrary relational particular y'. The third *explanandum* is the numerical distinctness of z, which is accounted for by the postulation of a third relational particular, identified with the numerical distinctness of z and so on, infinitely without an end.[44]

A pattern emerges. The second and third *explananda* are exactly of the same universal *type* – the numerical distinctness of an arbitrary relational particular (y and z, again, a formal ontological rather than an existence question). This type of *explanandum* is repeated an infinite number of times without a termination. The same universal type of *explanans* is equally repeated an infinite number of times: an arbitrary relational particular is identified with the numerical distinctness of another arbitrary relational particular. Thus, in each step after postulating y, the universal type of the *explanans* involves the universal type of the *explanandum*: the numerical distinctness of an arbitrary *relational* particular. Hence, nothing at all is explained about the global formal ontological problem of the numerical distinctness of relational particulars universally. It is just repeated infinitely without an end that the numerical distinctness is identified with an arbitrary relational particular. No step is taken forwards. Regarding the first *explanandum* of the numerical distinctness of *non-relational* particulars universally, one step is taken forwards by postulating y, which only leads to a vicious

---

[44] Note that x, y, and z are variables rather than the names of specific entities, and that this argument does not commit us to the existence of arbitrary objects discussed by structuralists in the philosophy of mathematics (see Horsten 2019: ch. 3).

infinite regress. Therefore, the first task of the global formal ontological explanation of the numerical distinctness of non-relational particulars fails, too. All in all, no numerical distinctness of any particular whatsoever is explained.

When numerical distinctness is not reified but is construed as an internal relation, the regress is halted at step 4; the numerical distinctness of x is not postulated as an entity. Construing numerical distinctness as an internal relation in the eliminativist sense does not therefore suffer from the same global metaphysical explanation failure as postulating numerical distinctness as an external relation – that is, as an additional entity to its relata. The internal-relation explanation is not threatened by this vicious infinite regress since entities themselves explain their distinctness, as will be seen in Section 4.2. It is then theoretically superior to its exclusive and exhaustive option, and we adopt it. Next, we will proceed to completing the internal-relation explanation of ontological forms in general.

4.2 Formal Ontological Relations and Ontological Form versus Being

4.2.1 Formal Ontological Relations, Their Reality, and Different Types

The ontological form of entities is their standing in a specific type of internal relations since these relations are character-neutral relations. Therefore, we draw a distinction between different types of internal relations. *Character-dependent internal relations* are those internal relations whose statements, if true, say something about the character of their relata even without further assumptions. Putative examples of the character-dependent type are provided by quantitative and qualitative comparisons, such as 'the mass of a Higgs boson is greater than the mass of an electron' and 'the blue of a navy blue is deeper than the blue of a light blue'. By contrast, *character-neutral internal relations* are internal relations whose statements, even if true, do not say anything about the character of their relata without further assumptions.

Earlier, we concluded that for an entity to have an ontological form is for it to be a relatum of a character-neutral type of internal relation or relations jointly in an order – for example, numerical distinctness. Thus, the suitable term for these ontological forms is, indeed, 'formal ontological relations'. Accordingly, true FOR statements do not tell us anything about the character of their relata without further assumptions. Rather, they describe the character-neutral relational way in which their relata exist. Hence, for an entity to have an ontological form is for it to be a relatum of a FOR or FORs jointly in an order. We may illustrate this by the example that for an entity to have the ontological form of being a part is for it to be the subject of the FOR of parthood.

Exact similarity, exact resemblance, similarity, and resemblance are therefore not FORs. Their statements as such do tell us something about the character of their relata. Let us assume that it is true that x exactly resembles y and we know it. This true statement as such tells us something about the character of x and y: they are exactly resembling; it could not be true without something being true about the character of x and y.

Consequently, a formal ontological distinction such as that between universals and particulars should not be made in terms of similarity or resemblance, which is our unique systematic reason to criticize D. C. Williams' (1986: 3) and Ehring's (2011: 32) way of making this distinction: particulars can be intrinsically exactly similar and numerically distinct, whereas universals cannot be such entities. Particulars do not obey the principle of the *identity of indiscernibles*, while universals do. Another way of making the distinction is that universals are capable of multiple locations as numerically identical whole entities, whereas particulars are not (for a recent defence, see Giberman 2021).

Both these accounts suffer from other serious problems. First, while being particulars, super-positioned micro-particles might have multiple locations (as wholes) at a time, which is a possibility that an account of particulars should not rule out a priori. Second, Rodriguez-Pereyra (2017) presents mutually exactly resembling universals and abstract particulars like numbers as counterexamples to Williams-Ehring distinction. Why should we rule out universals that do not obey the law of the identity of indiscernibles or particulars that obey it like numbers? For instance, if there is such an entity as number 12, it is not intrinsically exactly similar to any other entity, but it still might be considered an abstract particular (Rodriguez-Pereyra 2017: 622). The formal ontological way of distinguishing universals from particulars by the FOR of instantiation, familiar from the previous section, is not subject to these problems. It is, indeed, superior to these two competing accounts.

At this point, we can specify our earlier statement that there may be relational characters to distinguish relational characters from ontological form. There are two types of possible relational character: *internal relational character* and *external relational character*. The former is a character that entities have in virtue of being character-dependently internally related to something; two properties being exactly similar is a good example. Entities have an external relational character in virtue of being externally related to something, like possibly being two metres apart from each other. Ontological form differs even from internal relational character because the ontological form of an entity is its standing in character-neutral rather than character-dependent internal relations. Thus, ontological form is not what entities are like; rather, it is the way they exist.

On this basis, we are also able to draw a clear-cut distinction between formal ontological and other internally relational *terms*. Formal ontological terms are character-neutral internally relational terms, whereas other internally relational terms are character dependent: they occur in statements that in themselves say at least something about the character of the entities to which these terms apply. Moreover, formal ontological *terms* are *primitive* if they cannot be non-circularly defined. *Derivative* formal ontological *terms*, in turn, may be non-circularly defined. It depends on the metaphysical theory as to which formal ontological terms are primitive, and which are derivative. For instance, 'is a part of' is considered primitive and 'is a proper part of' derivative (and dyadic) in the metaphysical theories following the standard axiomatization of classical mereology.

Some ontological forms may be said to be *modal*, since some putative FORs are modal in nature. When we express these FORs by true character-neutral internally relational statements, these statements tell us how it is *necessary* or *possible* for an entity to be. For example, if x depends for its existence rigidly on y, then y's existence is necessary to the existence of x (or it is not possible for x to exist without y).

As internal relations, *FORs holding of actual entities are not entities* numerically distinct from their relata (see Lowe 2006: 46; Simons 2012: 138; Keinänen, Keskinen, & Hakkarainen 2019: ch. 2). Still, they may be said to be *real* in a sense: for something to be real is there to be a truth about it. Truth-bearers (you may pick up your favourite) are *true of* the relata of the actually holding FORs (whatever those FORs are) and these truths are in principle expressible by relational statements. To the relata of actually holding FORs, some formal ontological relational *terms* apply (no 'empty reference'). These FORs are *real but non-existing relatednesses of entities*. They do hold of their relata, which are entities standing in these character-neutral internal relations. This sense in which actually holding FORs are real differs from two other common technical senses of 'real' in analytic philosophy: that which exists is real, and that which is mind-independent in one way or another is real (as documented by Miller 2021). 'Real' employed here may be seen as an umbrella term covering at least (1) entities; (2) mind-independents; and (3) actually holding internal relations, which can cross-cut; this list is not intended to be exhaustive.

Now, for an entity to have an ontological form is for it to be a relatum of a FOR or FORs jointly in an order. Therefore, we can conclude that *the ontological form of entities is real* in the following sense: entities are relata of actually holding FORs although ontological forms are not entities. They do not exist in addition to the entities whose forms they are. Your heart, for example, really is a part of you even though being a part of is not an entity numerically distinct from you and your heart. In particular, ontological forms are not universal or general entities of any category such as instantiated relational universals or sets. Nevertheless, there can be truths of ontological forms and formal ontological terms that apply to entities. Our relational account of ontological form is *nominalist*. Our metatheory is not committed to the existence of universals although one may consistently endorse this theory and believe in some other universals than ontological forms and categories.

The holdings of FORs can be generically identical with each other although FORs are not entities that the flanking expressions could *designate* such as relational universals or sets. Neither do FORs have to be particular relational entities of which the flanking expressions are *true*. Generic identity does not equal the numerical identity of properties and is *non-factive*. Hence, the holdings of FORs can be generically identical with each other although these holdings are not entities of any category. *The generic identity of FORs is the sameness of the non-existing but real character-neutral relatednesses of entities.*

4.2.2 The Ground and Fundamentality of FORs

If FORs are character-neutral internal relations, why do they hold of their relata if they do? Why do entities have the ontological form that they have? To answer this question, we need to elaborate slightly on the sense in which FORs are internal. Due to their character neutrality, they cannot be internal in the 'property conception of internal relations', which is held by Armstrong, for instance (Keinänen, Keskinen, & Hakkarainen 2019: 521–5). The notion of character covers properties, which cannot then ground FORs as in the property conception. Instead, FORs are internal by the 'modified existential conception' of internal relations (Hakkarainen, Keinänen, & Keskinen 2018: 100; see Mulligan 1998: 344).

According to the modified existential conception, roughly, the mere *existence* of some entities is jointly sufficient and individually necessary for the holding of an internal relation (for a full account, see Hakkarainen 2018: 137–40). Their existence jointly necessitates and is individually necessary for the holding of the FOR. This is how it ought to be, given our view that FORs are character-neutral internal relations. For example, the existence of tropes necessitates the holding of numerical distinctness between them (Hakkarainen 2018: 145; see Section 5.2).

Of these *de re necessities*, one may in principle hold any of the following three alternative metaphysical views. Let us facilitate our expression and focus on the necessity of the holding of a FOR upon the existence of its relata (e.g., the numerical distinctness of tropes): (1) One may defend the view that this necessity is reducible to the existence of these entities in possible worlds, of which there are several accounts available in the literature (for a mapping of alternatives, see Divers 2002). For example, two tropes are numerically distinct in each possible world where they exist. (2) One may take the necessity in question as a primitive fact: it is just an inexplicable brute fact that the existence of the relata is sufficient for the holding of the FOR (e.g., the numerical distinctness of tropes). (3) One the grounds the necessity of the holding of a FOR in the formal ontological aspect of the non-modal essence of its relata: to stand in the FOR in an order is part of what it is to be the entity the relatum is. For example, Pippo necessarily stands in the FOR of numerical distinctness from Misu because to stand in it is part of what it is to be Pippo. As was seen in the previous section, Lowe holds this view. Although we are leaning towards the second, primitivist view, we do not want to take any firm stance on this issue here. We simply want to point out that our view of the ground of the necessary holding of FORs is available to the upholders of more than one modal metaphysics.

Elaborating on our account of FORs, we distinguish two types of them in a way that proves to be useful for the forthcoming discussion of fundamentality. Let us use Lowe's FORs of instantiation, characterization, and exemplification as illustrations of the two types of FORs: *fundamental* and *derived*. The holding of instantiation is not generically identical with the holding of any other FOR than instantiation; for Pippo to instantiate the kind cat is for him to instantiate the kind cat but nothing else in Lowe's system. This same circular uninformativeness holds of characterization. Instantiation and characterization are, indeed, fundamental FORs in Lowe's system.

Exemplification is another matter. For Pippo to exemplify regurgitating hairballs is for him to instantiate the kind cat *and* for the kind cat to be characterized by the attribute of regurgitating hairballs in this order of relations (Figure 4). A *third* relatum, the kind cat, is then brought into play, unlike in the case of instantiation and characterization. However, for Pippo to exemplify regurgitating hairballs is *neither* for him to instantiate the kind cat *nor* for the kind cat to be characterized by the attribute of regurgitating hairballs *individually*. Pippo's exemplification of regurgitating hairballs is generically identical with his instantiation of the kind cat and the kind cat being characterized by regurgitating hairballs in this order *jointly* but not *individually*. Notwithstanding the symmetry of generic identity, there holds *asymmetry* and *priority* here. The holdings of instantiation and characterization are individually prior to the holding of exemplification. Therefore, exemplification, in contrast to instantiation and characterization, is not a fundamental FOR in Lowe's system. Rather, its holding is *derivative* from the ordered joint holding of instantiation and

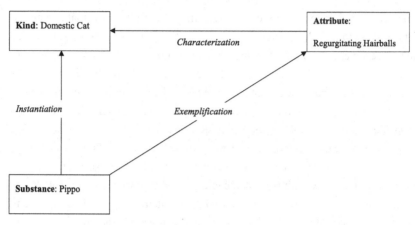

Figure 4 Pippo's exemplification of regurgitating hairballs

characterization in their respective orders: Pippo instantiates the kind that is characterized by the attribute. It is also decisive that the derivation requires the existence of a third entity: the kind. The instantiation and characterization are *non-circularly informative* of exemplification, as is required from derivativeness in addition to the order of asymmetry and priority (see Tahko 2018). A derivation base should be informative of the derived. By the notion of generic identity, we can account for the derivation or constitution of FORs, which Lowe leaves unexplained, as was seen earlier.

In general, we may say that *fundamental FORs* are such whose holding is not generically identical with any generically non-identical FORs, and the holding does not require any entity numerically distinct from the relata. By contrast, the holding of *derived FORs* is non-circularly and informatively generically identical with the ordered joint holding of generically non-identical FORs in their respective orders. The latter FORs are individually prior to the former FOR. It will turn out to be pivotal for non-fundamental categories that this derivation brings in entities numerically distinct from the relata of the derived FOR. Actually, the necessity of the existence of only one such additional entity for the holding of a FOR is sufficient for the FOR being derived. This distinction gets more support from its usefulness in explaining the fundamentality of ontological forms and categories in Section 5.1.1.

4.2.3 Distinguishing Ontological Form from Being

At this point, we can distinguish *ontological form* from *being* or *existence* in a determinate manner. The concept of *ontological form* is a complex concept consisting of the concepts of *form* and *being* or *existence*. Of form, we have a *nominalist relational* account. Accordingly, the concept of ontological form consists of the concept of FOR, that is, character-neutral internal relation and the notion of being or existence.

Regarding being and existence, we do not have to pursue several questions about them, such as their meaning or whether they are to be expressed by a quantifier or predicate. Suffice it that we simply make two assumptions about existence, leaving room for more than one view of it: (1) We follow the mainstream view in analytic metaphysics and metaontology that 'existence' and its cognates are interchangeable with 'being' and its cognates (van Inwagen 2009). (2) 'Existence' and 'being' are both univocal and existence or being is unified rather than modified. We assume *ontological monism*.

Characters of entities belong to the extension of the concept of being or existence in the metaphysical theories that are committed to the existence of characters – for example, realism about property universals, class or set nominalism, and trope nominalism.[45] The same holds of external relations (provided there are some) and the character that entities have in virtue of being externally related to something. If entities have essences numerically distinct from or identical to them, then essences are in the extension of 'being', too.

The upshot is that the totality of being consists of entities, including their characters and essences – if there are any. The ontological form of entities is generically identical with their standing in a character-neutral internal relation or relations jointly in an order. For example, you are, you exist, and your ontological forms consist of the FORs in which you stand in orders. Which FORs these are is an open formal ontological question, which differs from the question about your character: what you are like. Your existence is prior to your ontological forms in reality since the FORs in which you stand cannot hold without you existing. This may be called existentialism about ontological forms.

From this, it does not follow that being or existence is modified, which would be at odds with our ontological monism. Every entity is or exists in the same univocal sense; it is only that entities stand in different FORs. This standing does not modify their existence in any manner. For example, it does not literally modify your existence that arguably you depend for your existence on your brain specifically. We can explain away literal modes of being by our relational account of ontological form. We are formal ontologists without being mode of being theorists.

---

[45] It also follows that FORs do not have a character in this specific technical sense, because they do not exist.

4.3 Categories

4.3.1 Category Membership

Let us now apply our nominalist relationalism about ontological form to the perennial problem of categories and their existence and reality. We will propose a systematic solution to this problem: categories are, roughly, pluralities of entities sharing ontological forms. As such, categories are not identified with any distinct entity but are actual divisions of entities. We hold nominalist relationalism of categories, too.

To begin with, recall that one of the key insights of the formal ontological approach to metaphysics is that categories are analyzed by ontological forms. According to our account of ontological form, for an entity to have one is for it to be a relatum of a FOR or FORs jointly in an order. Hence, for an entity to be an entity of a category is for it to be a relatum of a FOR or FORs jointly in an order. Since being an entity of a category is being a member of that category, it follows that *for an entity to be a member of a category is for it to be a relatum of a FOR or FORs jointly in an order.* The membership of categories is generically identified with the entities' being the relata of a FOR or FORs jointly in the same order. As in Lowe's system, the order of a FOR might make a difference here. Entities may be the subjects or termini of a FOR, such as instantiation or proper parthood. If the order of a FOR is symmetry, then each of its relata stand trivially in the relation in the same order.

Thus, the FOR or FORs holding of entities determine the membership of entities in categories: entities standing in the same FOR or FORs in the same order belong to the same category. This is a *relational* view influenced by Lowe and Simons (see Section 3) that contrasts with McDaniel's (2017: 122–7) view of categories as modes of being that are not necessarily relational. Consequently, entity or being is not a category because the membership determination of categories by a FOR or FORs jointly *presupposes* entities or beings. However, this is how it ought to be. Categories are categories of entities or beings. The category of entities or beings would be then circular: the category of entities of entities. The concept of entity or being is *transcendental* in Medieval terms: it transcends categories (Goris & Aertsen 2019: ch. 1).

In contrast to categories, the membership of highly general types of entities that are not categories – natural kinds in particular – is not generically identical with the entities standing in a FOR or FORs jointly in the same order; it is determined in some other way. For example, it is beyond reasonable doubt that the membership of the kind electron or *funghi porcini* is not generically identical with standing in a FOR or FORs jointly in an order. Membership determination in the sense of generic identity by FORs distinguish categories from non-categorial highly general types of entities such as natural kinds (if there are any). This is our solution of the cut-off point problem about distinguishing categories from other kind of highly general types of entities (see Section 3).[46]

Thus, each category is construed as a group of those entities that stand in the same FOR or FORs jointly in the same order. We consider these groups *pluralities* of entities, which is close to a view defended by Lowe. One must not understand this as the identification of categories with pluralities; we do not numerically identify categories with anything. We do not consider pluralities individuals and numerical identity is not a one-to-many relation. Rather, there just are pluralities of entities that are relata of the same FOR or FORs jointly in the same order.[47]

Although our relational account builds upon Lowe and Simons, it differs from their views for three reasons. First, we have a different account of FORs than Lowe and he does not have an account of the constitution of FORs. Second, we do not hold a view of analyzing categories by factors like Simons. Another difference from Lowe's view is that according to his strong essentialism, categorial differences hold ultimately in virtue of the non-modal essences of entities, whereas we think that for an entity to be a member of a category is for it to stand in a FOR or FORs jointly in an order, which might a brute fact. In our account, categories are construed as pluralities of existing beings with the same character-neutral internally relational way of existence. Our account is not committed to Lowe's strong essentialism about formal ontology; our commitments are more moderate. A formal ontologist does not need to be a serious or non-modal essentialist.

4.3.2 Existence and Reality of Categories

Earlier, we concluded that as internal relations, FORs are not additional entities to their relata. Thus, they do not force us to make categories entities numerically distinct from their members. Our conclusion is therefore that categories do not exist as additional entities to their members. There are members of categories but there are not categories as numerically distinct entities of any kind, neither

---

[46] We disagree then with James Miller's recent proposed solution to the cut-off point problem. According to Miller (2022: ch. 6), a necessary condition for an ontological category is that its full definition involves essential dependence relations between it and other categories, whereas 'ordinary categories' require only existential dependence relations. As will be seen in Section 5.1.2, Miller's proposal cannot capture some category theories, such as Seibt's process ontology and trope theories that are not committed to essential dependence relations.

[47] Due to space restrictions, we simply assume here that the existence of pluralities is nothing but the existence of their members and hence pluralities are not individuals. Therefore, it makes sense to speak about the existence of pluralities because it makes sense to speak about the existence of their members.

as universals (kinds or properties), as sums, as classes, as sets, nor as tropes or modes. The falling of entities under a category is generically identical with their standing in the same FOR or FORs in the same order. There is no need to assume categories as entities in addition to their members.

Furthermore, if one held that categories were relational entities numerically distinct from their members, then one's view might be threatened by a vicious infinite regress – as was seen earlier in the case of the external-relation account for ontological forms. Thus, categories are neither universals nor particulars, on which Lowe (2006: 43) and Simons (2012: 131, 138) agree.[48] Here we disagree, for instance, with Smith, who is a realist about categories (see Section 3). Our view is *nominalist* about categories: there are no categories as universal or general entities of any sort.

From this, it does not follow that categories are mere conceptual or linguistic constructions. First of all, we do not identify categories with concepts or terms. Second, an entity's standing in some FOR or FORs to something in an order can be – and, in most metaphysical theories nowadays, is claimed to be – mind-independent. Nonetheless, category membership can be determined mind dependently in at least some cases; our account as such does not rule out the FOR of ontological dependence on mind being a determining relation of a category. Third, recall that we argued earlier that actual FORs are *real* in a sense. They hold of their relata because they may be expressed, in principle, by *true* character-neutral internally relational statements. Since actual FORs determine (in the sense of generic identity) the membership of categories, any analysis, definition, or characterization of a category is to be given by a FOR or FORs jointly including their order. Therefore, actual categories are also in principle expressible by true, character-neutral, internally relational statements. In them, certain terms apply to the entities of the category or categories in question although categories are not identified with terms or concepts. This is another nominalist element of our view.[49] Hence, actual categories may be said to be *real*, although they are not entities numerically distinct from their members. It is true that they have members, and the membership is determined by a FOR or FORs in an order. In Lowe's system, for instance, those entities are kinds of which it holds true that they are instantiated and characterized by numerically distinct entities. To these entities and only them, 'being a kind' applies.

---

[48] For arguments supporting this view within Lowe's four-category ontology, see Lowe (2006: ch. 3.3).

[49] We are capable of talk about categories, and that kind of talk is general. Thus, what is ultimately needed is some plausible account of the truth conditions of sentences that are used to make assertions about categories. Developing such an account is beyond the scope of this Element.

We have then argued for a *nominalist relationalism about categories*. If our account is correct, formal ontology has a *real* subject matter – that is, real ontological forms and categories – even if it does not have distinctly *existing* objects of study. It is the task of the formal ontologist, not the task of the metametaphysician – whose hat we are wearing here – to answer the questions of what the categories and their relations are, and how they are to be analyzed or defined by FORs and their order.

5 What Can We Do with Our Metatheory?

5.1 Formal Ontological Fundamentality vs Non-fundamentality

5.1.1 Our Proposal

The literature on grounding has resulted in a discussion on metaphysical fundamentality of late (Tahko 2018). This discussion has focused almost exclusively on *ontological* fundamentality: the fundamentality of entities. Fundamentality of the ontological forms and categories of entities, that is, *formal ontological* fundamentality has been practically ignored. Next, we shall show how we can make a proposal about formal ontological fundamentality and non-fundamentality based on our metatheory of formal ontology. Our focus will be on categorial fundamentality/non-fundamentality. In a nutshell, fundamental categories are determined by fundamental FORs, whereas at least one non-fundamental FOR plays a part in the case of non-fundamental categories. Our proposal displays the fertility of our metatheory for metaphysics. We leave the relation between formal ontological and ontological fundamentality for future research due to space restrictions.

Before proceeding to our proposal, we need to make two remarks about categorial fundamentality and non-fundamentality. First, categorial posteriority is not *subsumption*: non-fundamental categories are not necessarily subsumed under fundamental categories. In many nominalist or realist bundle theories of objects, objects constitute a non-fundamental category and tropes or property universals form the fundamental category. Yet it is not correct to say in these theories that objects are subsumed under tropes or property universals since objects in general are not tropes or universals in them. Second, the distinction between fundamental and non-fundamental categories presupposes that entities divide into more than one category since it is arguably an exclusive distinction. No entity can be a member of both a fundamental and a non-fundamental category. Therefore, this distinction does not apply to theories where the relevant category distinction is not necessarily exclusive (e.g., trope theories by Williams 1953 and Campbell 1990) or one-category formal ontologies like

Paul's (2017) mereological bundle theory and Seibt's (2018) process theory. According to Paul and Seibt, there are entities of one category only. We can set aside these category theories here.

Earlier, we distinguished fundamental FORs from the derived. Derivation of FORs involves non-circular informativeness and the order of asymmetry and priority. We may therefore say that to have a *fundamental ontological form* is to stand in a fundamental FOR or FORs jointly in an order, whereas to have a *non-fundamental ontological form* is to stand in at least one derived FOR in an order. We have also argued that categories are analyzed by ontological forms that are standings in FORs in an order. Consequently, *fundamental categories* are analyzed by a fundamental FOR or FORs jointly in an order and *non-fundamental categories* are analyzed by at least one derived FOR in an order. The holding of a derived FOR is non-circularly and informatively generically identical to the ordered joint holding of some fundamental FORs in their orders (symmetry, asymmetry, non-symmetry). It is also decisive that a derived FOR requires the existence of at least one entity numerically distinct from the relata of the FOR, as in the case of Lowe's exemplification there must be a kind or mode. The necessity of the existence of such an entity for the holding of a FOR is sufficient for the FOR being derived. Accordingly, the ontological form of a member of a non-fundamental category also derives from the ontological form of at least one entity numerically distinct from the member.

In the case of non-fundamental categories, it is then sufficient for making a category non-fundamental that it is analyzed *at least partly* by a derived FOR in an order. This leaves it open that fundamental FORs may be involved in the analysis. Take for instance the numerical identity of the members of non-fundamental categories such as objects in some bundle theories. Numerical identity is a good candidate for a fundamental FOR and it seems to be at play in the analysis of objects in these theories because objects are supposed to have numerical identity. By contrast, fundamental categories must be analyzed by fundamental FORs *fully*. It might be possible that a single FOR in an order is the sole analysans like the FOR of instantiation for universals and particulars.

On this basis, we can conclude that categorial *fundamentality* is being fully analyzed by a fundamental FOR or FORs jointly in an order and categorial *non-fundamentality* is being at least partly analyzed by a derived FOR in an order (in terms of generic identity). The members of fundamental categories stand in the same fundamental FOR or FORs jointly in the same order, and their membership of a fundamental category is nothing more. Take any member of a fundamental category; it is a relatum of the same fundamental FOR or FORs in the same order as any other member of the category and nothing else *qua* the member of this category. By contrast, take any member of a non-fundamental category; it is a relatum of the same derived and possibly fundamental FOR or FORs jointly in the same order as any other member of that category. The holding of the derived FOR or FORs require the existence of at least one entity numerically distinct from the member.

5.1.2 Analyzing Formal Ontologies in Terms of Our Proposal

This proposal of categorial fundamentality and non-fundamentality has a perfect fit with Lowe's and Smith's neo-Aristotelian theories of categories in which the four common fundamental categories are analyzed by the fundamental FORs of instantiation and characterization or inherence. It fits equally with Heil's (2012) and C. B. Martin's (1980) nominalist systems of substances and modes, which are roughly Lowe's theory without universals. In their case, only characterization or inherence is needed. Our proposal gets further confirmation from some non-Aristotelian contemporary formal ontologies, such as perdurantism and trope theory: it can capture their account of fundamental and non-fundamental categories. This is revealed by a short formal ontological analysis of them, although most of these theories are not formulated formal ontologically.

Consider first those non-holist theories in which entities of a non-fundamental category are wholes composed of proper parts. A well-known example is simple *perdurantism*: persisting objects as perdurants are wholes of temporal parts (Figure 5). As Lewis (1986: 202) puts it: 'Something *perdures* iff it persists by having different temporal parts, or stages, at different times, though no one part of it is wholly present at more than one time.' For example,

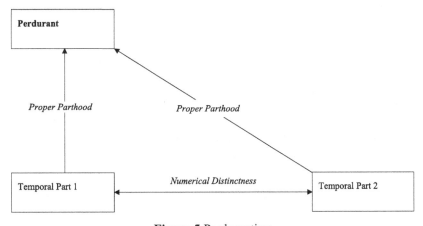

Figure 5 Perdurantism

Pippo is a whole of temporal parts, which are Pippo at each time of his existence (Hawley 2001: 42). A perdurant is then composed of at least two mereologically disjoint temporal parts, which are the proper parts of the perdurant; proper parts are numerically distinct from their whole. Proper parthood is standardly considered dyadic, so it holds between a temporal part and a perdurant. Hence, it can hold in perdurantism only if there is at least *another* temporal part bearing numerical distinctness to the first and proper parthood to the perdurant. The first temporal part being a proper part of the perdurant requires the existence of the other temporal part. Recall that it is sufficient for a FOR being derived that its holding requires the existence of an entity numerically distinct from the relata of the FOR (e.g., Lowe's exemplification). Thus, proper parthood between any temporal part and the perdurant is a derived FOR. We leave it to the perdurantists to fill in the details about its derivation.

The upshot is that perdurants constitute a non-fundamental category in perdurantism, as they should be since their category is partly analyzed by the derived FOR of proper parthood. This result applies equally to any categorization of entities as four-dimensional objects composed of temporal parts, such as processes as a non-fundamental category in some views of processes (see e.g., Lowe 2006: 80–1; Simons 2012: 135). It also applies to those bundle theories of objects or substances according to which objects or substances are wholes of at least two particular or universal natures and proper parthood is dyadic. Our trope theory is one of them (see Section 5.2).

In Jaegwon Kim's property-exemplification view of *events*, they form a non-fundamental category constituted of an object x, a property P, and a time t (Kim 1993: ch. 3). An event is x's having P at t. For example, the event of Pippo regurgitating hairballs at 9 am is Pippo's having the property of regurgitating hairballs at 9 am. The event of object x's having property P at time t exists if and only if the object x has P at a given time. Events are numerically identical if and only if they have the same constituents of the same category (Kim 1993: ch. 3). When Kim's account is put in terms of our metatheory, we can say that the FOR of constitution holding from an object, a property, or a moment of time to an event should be a derived FOR. The decisive point is the same as with perdurantism: the holding of this FOR requires an extra entity (a property, moment, or object). The consequence is the wanted one: events form a non-fundamental category because for an entity to be an event is *partly* for it to be a relatum of the derived FOR of constitution from a property, moment, or an object to the event.

Concrete objects are the sole fundamental category in Reism (see Kotarbiński 1955; Woleński 2020). They may be considered countable concrete individuals, which stand in the FOR of numerical distinctness to all other objects. Objects can be complex (i.e., have proper parts), such as rubber balls, or simple (e.g., electrons), but the FOR of parthood does not figure in the analysis of the category of objects. Objects can be endowed with a complex nature in the sense of having a set of distinct features, but it depends on the specific version of Reism whether one gives any further metaphysical account of this. For instance, one may attempt to account for the prima facie distinct features of objects by means of their resemblances (as in Rodriguez-Pereyra 2002). Rodriguez-Pereyra (2002) has introduced sets as an additional fundamental category to solve certain problems of his account. In his system, objects stand in the fundamental FOR of membership to sets.[50]

All in all, our proposal of the fundamental/non-fundamental categories distinction gets confirmation from several different formal ontologically analyzed theories. Are there any problematic cases for it? Given what we said about non-holist views, one might suggest that holist theories like Jonathan Schaffer's priority monism (2009, 2010a, 2010b) create a problem for our account since entities of the fundamental category are wholes rather than proper parts in holism. However, it does not have to be so. Our account is flexible enough to accommodate Schaffer's priority monism. The crucial point is that in Schaffer's construal proper parthood does not analyze the fundamental category of substances, which has only one member. Rather, the only substance is the sole *part* of the actual material cosmos and the only ontologically independent (ungrounded) entity (Schaffer 2010a: 344, 2010b: 5, 38). Unlike proper parthood, parthood is standardly taken reflexive. Thus, its holding does not require any numerically distinct entity from the substance or cosmos. Therefore, parthood does not have to be a derived FOR. The category of substances can be fundamental just like Schaffer proposes.

Grounding we may set aside here since it does not hold reflexively of the ungrounded substance, and it is not a FOR: it is the relation of the inheritance of existence rather than an ontological form in Schaffer's view (2010b). Every other entity than the only substance inherits its existence ultimately from the ungrounded substance (Schaffer 2016a: 95, 2010b: 62). These other entities, like we human beings, are 'partialia', which form the non-fundamental category (Schaffer 2009: 379, 2010b: 47). The defining feature of *partialia* is that they are proper parts of the substance (Schaffer 2010a: 347, 2010b: 42). There must be more than one of them, given there is one, and these proper parts are mereologically disjoint (Schaffer 2010a: 356). Thus, a *partiale* cannot bear dyadic proper parthood to the substance without there being another *partiale*. Take any *partiale*

---

[50] Reism or a two-category ontology of objects and sets is nowadays often called 'nominalism' or even 'classical nominalism' (Rodriguez-Pereyra 2019), ostrich nominalism (Devitt 1980) and resemblance nominalism (Rodriguez-Pereyra 2002) serving as current examples.

and its being a proper part of the substance requires the existence of another *partiale*. Proper parthood is a derived FOR that defines *partialia* in Schaffer's monism. In our analysis, it renders *partialia* a non-fundamental category.[51]

5.2 Our Metatheory and Our Trope Theory

The fecundity of our metatheory of formal ontology and account of the distinction between fundamental and non-fundamental categories gets even more support from how it helps us to precisely state the formal ontology in our Strong Nuclear Theory of tropes, substances, and the relation of inherence between them ('SNT', for short). Like Williams' paradigmatic trope theory, the SNT construes a one-category trope theory and analyzes inherence in more transparent terms following the formal ontological approach to metaphysics. All fundamental entities are tropes and objects are constructed by means of tropes fulfilling certain conditions. The SNT constitutes a formal ontologically economical alternative to other category systems striving to solve the same central metaphysical problems, such as the problem of universals and the problem of intrinsic change of concrete particulars (see Keinänen & Hakkarainen 2010; Keinänen 2011). The SNT and its defence against the counter-arguments to trope theory in the literature cannot be fully captured without understanding the ontological and formal ontological description of tropes in the SNT (Hakkarainen 2018). Our metatheory provides an illuminating tool for that.

Ontologically, tropes are entities that are standardly identified with characters or natures: what tropes are like. Plausible examples of tropes or characters in scientifically informed metaphysics are determinate basic quantities: rest masses, charges, and spin quantum numbers. These characters are 'thin' or qualitatively simple: they do not even have different aspects that would be numerically identical with them. They can also be intrinsically indiscernible and numerically distinct; the ontological principle of the identity of indiscernibles does not hold true of tropes.

Our focus is on the *ontological form* of tropes, rather than their ontology. Let us consider the definitions of the *terms* of FORs in the SNT first. There are two *primitive* FORs *qua* terms: numerical identity and parthood. They are not defined in the SNT. One of the *defined* FORs *qua* terms in it, numerical distinctness, is defined as the negation of numerical identity. Another defined

---

[51] Armstrong's factualism is another theory in which complex entities form the fundamental category, at least on one reading (Armstrong 1997: 20, 28, 131). We do not discuss Armstrong's factualism since its supposedly fundamental category of facts or states of affairs is not transparent enough for a formal ontological analysis (Keinänen, Hakkarainen, & Keskinen 2016).

FOR term, proper parthood, is defined by numerical identity and parthood: x is a proper part of $y=_{df} x$ is a part of y AND x is not numerically identical with y.

The third defined FOR term is strong rigid (existential) dependence that is defined modally by the notion of existence, numerical identity, and parthood. A *contingent* entity x is strongly *rigidly* dependent on a *contingent* entity y if and only if

(1) it is not possible that x exists, and y does not exist
(2) x and y are not numerically identical
(3) y is not a part of x (see Keinänen 2011: 431).

Let us proceed to FORs as real *relatednesses of entities* rather than terms; recall that FORs are not terms or concepts. The *numerical identity* of tropes is not only a primitive term but also their *fundamental* and reflexive FOR in the SNT. The holding of the FOR of numerical identity of each trope is not generically identical with any other FOR. The only explanation for the holding of numerical identity of each trope is the mere existence of the trope: it is an inexplicable brute fact that each trope has numerical identity. This involves that each trope is a unity (i.e., one and countable) and an individual.

Another fundamental and reflexive FOR in the SNT is *parthood* that holds of every trope: each trope is a part. Consider any trope whatsoever and its sole existence is sufficient and necessary for it being a part. According to the SNT, however, no trope is a whole. The SNT states that tropes are mereologically simple: mereological atoms. This ontological form distinguishes tropes fundamentally from modes in Lowe's four-category ontology, for instance. Lowe denies that a mode is a part of the object that it characterizes (2006: 97).

As we argued earlier, for an entity to have a fundamental ontological form is for it to be a relatum of a fundamental FOR or FORs jointly in an order. Therefore, the holding of both numerical identity and reflexive parthood is a fundamental ontological form of tropes. Their joint holding is generically identical with the *full* fundamental ontological form of tropes. Fundamentally, in formal ontological terms, *tropes are individual simple parts*, which is then the definition of the *fundamental* category of tropes in the SNT.

Recall that our metatheory allows for *derived* ontological forms for the members of any fundamental category if these forms do not define the category. In the SNT, some *derived* FORs also hold of tropes. Let us consider two examples. First, every trope is necessarily a *proper part* of a substance: there are no 'free-floating tropes' (Figure 6). To expound the constitution of the relation of proper parthood between tropes and substances, let us first facilitate the presentation and take the example of an arbitrary minimal substance. Such a substance is a simple substance since it does not have parts that are substances;

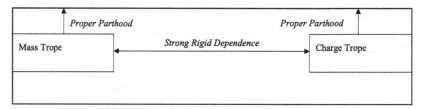

Figure 6 Arbitrary minimal substance with two nuclear tropes

it has only two trope parts, say, a rest mass trope and a charge trope. It is composed of the minimal number of parts and therefore it is a minimal substance. Let us also assume that the two tropes are mutually *strongly rigidly dependent*: neither of them can exist without the other. In other words, they are the *nuclear tropes* of the simple substance and its only tropes. Consequently, their plurality must also exist given the contingent existence of one of them.

According to the SNT, every plurality of tropes that contains, first, all tropes rigidly dependent on certain nuclear trope(s), and second, a nuclear trope or nuclear tropes satisfying these rigid dependencies constitutes an individual. Thus, the plurality of the rest mass and charge tropes constitutes an individual, which is a mereological sum of these tropes closed under strong rigid dependencies among the tropes: a dependence closure of the tropes. By the transitivity of rigid dependence, this individual itself is not rigidly dependent on any entity that is not its proper part, it is a *strongly independent particular*, a simple substance.[52] All its constituent tropes are strongly rigidly dependent on the individual (simple substance). Were this individual strongly rigidly dependent on tropes that are not its parts, also its constituent tropes would be strongly rigidly dependent on these additional tropes (by the transitivity). This would contradict the assumption that these tropes already form a dependence closure with respect to strong rigid dependence.

Regarding the relation of proper parthood holding between the arbitrary minimal substance and its two mutually strongly rigidly dependent trope parts (the rest mass and charge), the upshot is that the *holding* of proper parthood from one of the tropes to the substance requires the existence of the other trope. This result generalizes in the SNT. Thus, proper parthood from any trope to a simple substance is a *derived* FOR. The same holds of any simple substance, which makes substances a non-fundamental category in the SNT, in the same manner as in our analysis of perdurants. It is a defining feature of substances in the SNT that they are wholes. It also follows that the FOR of proper parthood between a trope

---

[52] *Strongly independent particulars* are not strongly rigidly dependent on any mereologically disjoint entities. We assume simply here that every plurality of tropes forming a dependence closure of tropes constitutes an individual.

and a simple substance is not a fundamental ontological form of any trope in the SNT, in contrast to the parthood reflexively holding of tropes. Since the onto-logical form of a trope is specified without recourse to proper parthood, no trope is *fundamentally* a proper part of a substance (in formal ontological terms).

Second, *concreteness* is another derived ontological form of each trope. According to the SNT, every trope is located in space-time. This entails that no trope is abstract, that is, an entity not having even a temporal location. Nevertheless, we leave the details to some other occasion. The derived status of concreteness and proper parthood does not mean, however, that no trope is *necessarily* concrete and a proper part. Contrastingly, the SNT states that every trope is necessarily concrete and a proper part of some simple substance.[53]

Let us take nuclear tropes as an example of proper parthood (bracketing the limiting case of singular nuclear tropes). Necessarily, if there is an arbitrary nuclear trope, then there is another trope or there are other tropes, and these tropes are strongly rigidly dependent on each other. Since this trope is a part of a plurality of tropes forming a dependence closure, it follows that the arbitrary trope is also necessarily a proper part of a simple substance. Equally, any arbitrary trope exists necessarily at a spatio-temporal location. The concreteness of every trope and proper parthood between an arbitrary nuclear trope and a simple substance are *necessary* derived FORs in the SNT, just like a substance necessarily and derivately exemplifies its essential attributes in Lowe's system (e.g., Pippo's exemplification of regurgitating hairballs). However, the derived status of concreteness and proper parthood does not make tropes a non-fundamental category in the SNT, just like exemplification does not make substances a non-fundamental category in Lowe's system. As was seen just, the SNT does not define the fundamental category of tropes by these derived FORs, whereas it defines the non-fundamental category of sub-stances partly by the derived FOR of proper parthood.

5.3 What Is Metaphysics?

5.3.1 General Metaphysics

Armed with our metatheory and learning from Aristotle and the metaphysical tradition, we can finish by proposing a *unifying* formal ontological view of the subject matter, general questions, and branches of metaphysics, and their inter-relations. Tentatively, when one asks, 'what is it to be?', one is doing general metaphysics that divides into ontology and formal ontology. In ontology, one asks what there is and why, whereas formal ontology studies ontological forms and

---

[53] Another distinguishing component of the SNT is that every trope is necessarily strongly rigidly dependent, which we do not discuss here due to space restrictions (see Keinänen 2011).

categories. General metaphysics is logically prior to formal ontology that is equally prior to ontology.

To begin with, let us draw inspiration from the philosopher who gave the first known systematic account about metaphysics in the Western tradition. According to Aristotle, as is well-known, the first philosophy, later termed metaphysics, investigates *being as being* (Aristotle 1958: 1003a 21).[54] In Greek, 'being as being' is *to on hê on*, which means more literally 'that which is, in so far as it is something that is'. Aristotle thinks that the *object of consideration* of metaphysics is *to on*: being in the sense of *that which is*. Recall that this is 'being' in the *thing sense*. It covers being*s*, like Pippo, Misu, and we (things), and their totality (everything). To this object of consideration, Aristotle adds: 'what belongs to this in virtue of itself [*kath' hauto*]' (Aristotle 1958: 1003a 21; translation Politis 2004: 90). Accordingly, metaphysics also considers that which belongs *essentially* to being in the thing sense (Aristotle 1958: 1003a 21).

Aristotle captures the metaphysical *perspective* to being in the thing sense by the phrase *hê on*: 'in so far as it is something that is' (Politis 2004: 91). Here we have the most abstract perspective in which being in the thing sense and what is essential to it are considered apart from the more specific features of beings. This perspective consists in what all beings share: being in the *state* sense. Pippo, Misu, and we, for instance, share the state of being since we are there.

Accordingly, Vasilis Politis (2004: 2) claims that Aristotle's *basic question* in *Metaphysics* is: *what is being*? As such, the English phrase of 'what is being?' can reasonably be read in two ways. Due to the perspective of metaphysics, the first reading is '*what is it for something, anything to be?*' (see Politis 2004: 90). This may be understood as a question about the essence, nature, and/or definition of being *itself* in the state sense. Its linguistic or conceptual *meaning* and the proper way to *express* it are distinct issues from it. The question also involves the problem about the possible *features of being* in the state sense, such as its relation to other conceivable things in the vicinity: existence, subsistence, becoming, being real, and their opposites, such as non-being and inexistence. This relation may take several forms like numerical identity, distinctness, fundamentality, derivation, and modification: there are several different views about the relation between, say, being and existence in the history of metaphysics. Meinong, for instance, considers existence a mode of being, as was seen earlier.

'What is it to be?' looks like an Aristotelian question asking for the real definition of the real essence of being in the state sense. However, this question does not presuppose Aristotelian essentialism, not to speak about Aristotelian

---

[54] We refer to Aristotle by the standard Bekker numbering rather than page numbers.

substance metaphysics, since it can be abstracted from Aristotelianism. We only propose that 'what is it to be?' is *the primary question of general metaphysics* and point out that it and the answers to it are at the outset open to different construals. Indeed, there have been several alternative conceptions of them. General metaphysics is the field of philosophy addressing this primary question and the problems about the relation of being to existence, becoming, and so on.

Another point to be appreciated is that when asking what it is to be, one does not have to assume that being in the state sense is itself an entity, in the category of, say, properties, to which every other entity is somehow related. Indeed, it seems reasonable not to reify being in the state sense. Nonetheless, it can be construed as real in the sense that there are true existentials, such as 'Pippo is there' (it is another issue, which we do not touch upon, why they are true). If one reified being in the state sense, one should show that the reification does not lead to a vicious infinite regress of being entities: being itself as an entity, the being of that entity as a distinct entity and so on and so forth. Of course, this gives rise to the reasonable follow-up question: *what* are we then talking about when we are talking about being in the state sense? We are back to the question with which we started: what is it to be? All these are metaphysical matters, which need not be settled in this specific metametaphysical context.

Our proposal is close to Nicolai Hartmann's (2019: 51) insightful 'problem of being' (*Seinsproblem* in German) from the 1920s and 1930s in the early twentieth-century new ontology in German. With him, we share the starting point in being as being in Aristotle. Hartmann considers being that is shared by all the beings (Hartmann 2019: 53–4). He adopts Aristotle's 'formula' of being as being for the reason that 'because it considers what is [being in the thing sense] only insofar as it is, thus, only in its most universal aspect, it indirectly comes across "being" [in the state sense: *Sein*] over and above "what is" nonetheless' (Hartmann 2019: 53).

As was seen earlier, it is at least conceivable that beings *are in different ways*: their being literally has different modifications, which are features of being in the state sense. For example, one conceivable possibility is that contingent being is a mode of being (e.g., Vallicella 2014). It differs from the mode of necessary being (Vallicella 2014). Pippo's contingent being is literally modified in one way, the possible necessary being of number 1 in another. This ontological pluralism consists in the affirmative answer to the questions: *Is being modified*? *Does it have modes*? The negative answer is ontological monism. We suggest that this is *the secondary question of general metaphysics*.

Another possible feature of being in the state sense consists in its *principles*. Some historical philosophers have considered the principles of contradiction

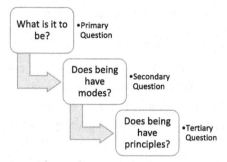

Figure 7 Basic questions of general metaphysics

and sufficient reason or ground the principles of being itself (e.g., Baumgarten 2013: 100, 105). Accordingly, we think that the tertiary question of general metaphysics is: *does being have principles* (Figure 7)?

General metaphysics consists then in considering being in the state sense and its features: its unitarity or plurality (modifications), principles and relation to existence, subsistence, becoming, being real, and their opposites. No belief about the being of anything, however specific, can avoid presupposing something about these general metaphysical matters due to their nature concerning being as such. Since Quine (1948), the dominant metaphysical supposition has been that being, existence, and being real are one and the same, equally fundamental, and unitary, or at least that their terms are interchangeable (see van Inwagen 2009).

Our proposal about general metaphysics resembles a scholastic Aristotelian view of metaphysics that has stood the test of time well. Following Avicenna (990–1037), many Latin authors from the thirteenth century onwards distinguish general metaphysics as the universal science of being as being from theology as the special science of being considering a specific entity, namely, God, even though Aristotle called the first philosophy 'theology' in *Metaphysics 6* (Epsilon) (Darge 2014: 92–3; Goris & Aertsen 2019: sec. 6; Lamanna 2021). We will follow this classic distinction between general metaphysics and theology, in which theology as a branch of metaphysics may be construed as a special metaphysics.

5.3.2 Ontology and Formal Ontology

The second reading of 'what is being?' is generated by the thing sense of 'being', which is the object of consideration of metaphysics in Aristotle. *Which are those that are?* Since metaphysics is not only a descriptive field of study of being as being but also already in Aristotle an explanatory one, we can add to this the question *why* entities are there. An inescapable metaphysical

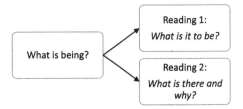

Figure 8 Two readings of the basic question

problem in plain English is: *what is there and why* (Figure 8)?[55] 'Primary being' (*protê ousia*, often simply *ousia*) is Aristotle's term for those beings that answers the why question (Politis 2004: 10). Nowadays, metaphysicians prefer to speak about the grounds of entities or fundamental entities rather than primary being, which is a practice we shall follow.

We propose that the primary *ontological question* is: *what are beings or entities and their grounds?* Here we use 'ontological' and 'ontology' in the familiar Quinean sense: study of what there is.[56] We only extend it to the consideration of the possible ground of entities. In our proposal, then, ontology is the branch of metaphysics considering questions, *what is there and on what ground?* Ontology involves the problems what fundamental and non-fundamental entities are, relatively or absolutely, and how they relate to each other (given there are any), which have been lately discussed in the literature on metaphysical grounding and fundamentality (see Tahko 2018). Accordingly, metaphysical grounding is more precisely an ontological concept, as well as ontological fundamentality (see Section 5.1.1).

Ontology also covers questions such as what exists and what is real since general metaphysical (pre-)suppositions about being in relation to existence and reality have implications for the question-setting of ontology. After Quine (1948), typically 'what is there?', 'what exists?', and 'what is real?' are considered interchangeable. Nowadays a paradigmatic ontological problem is

---

[55] Consequently, '*why is there something rather than nothing?*' is also an ontological question (by e.g., Leibniz 1989: 210).

[56] 'Ontologia' is an early seventeenth-century Latin neologism coming from the Greek *ontos*, which is the possessive of 'being', and *logos*, which means 'study' or 'doctrine' (Lamanna 2014; Smith 2022). 'Ontologia' has a different use from the Quinean parlance. This different use originates in the seventeenth-century German Protestant conception of ontology as general metaphysics building upon the scholastic distinction between general metaphysics and theology, especially in Francisco Suárez (1548–1617) (Lamanna 2014, 2021). Hartmann comes close to it (2019: 54). In that *ontos* is understood as meaning being as being (Lamanna 2014: 147), whereas in the Quinean use, being is considered a being or the totality of beings. As was seen in Section 2.1, the third use of ontology is Husserl's conception of it as the a priori science of the essence of possible objects as such. It has affinities with Wolff's understanding of ontology or the first philosophy as the science of possible and actual beings (Hettche & Dyck 2019: sec. 5).

whether there are *abstract objects* (numbers, sets, properties, or propositions in particular) rather than, for example, gravitational waves (van Inwagen & Sullivan 2021: sec. 4). In the Quinean tradition, this is taken to be interchangeable with the problem whether abstract objects exist: ontological problems are considered existence questions (van Inwagen & Sullivan 2021: sec. 4).

We think that ontology also includes different problems about the essence, properties, and nature or character of entities if these are reified as, say, attributes, modes, tropes, sets, or propositions. Then these problems are or involve ontological problems about what there is: essences, properties, and natures or characters as entities of some categories. For example, why existing quantities form kinds such as the charge and mass of the electron is an ontological problem.

As pointed out in Section 2, ontological form may in principle be understood as mode of being: an ontological form literally modifies being. A formal ontologist can answer this secondary general metaphysical question about being modifying or not in the affirmative. Ingarden is such a formal ontologist. However, as we have argued, that is not necessary; our answer is negative. On our account, an ontological form is not a mode of being although it is a relational feature of an entity and hence a metaphysical matter. The *primary formal ontological question whether beings have ontological forms* is therefore a metaphysical question but logically independent from the affirmative answer to the secondary general metaphysical question.

As a branch of metaphysics, formal ontology is principally the one investigating ontological forms. Regarding them, we have problems of both their definition and reality (actually holding FORs): *how are they analyzed, which of them are real*? These questions can concern only one, some, or all ontological forms. Since categories and their distinctions are analyzed by ontological forms, formal ontology studies categories, too. The *secondary formal ontological questions* are then: *how are categories analyzed* and *which are they and their relations*? These analyzing questions also concern *putative* ontological forms and categories since formal ontology considers them (see Section 5.3.3).

5.3.3 Unifying Metaphysics by General Metaphysics and Formal Ontology

Accordingly, we propose that general metaphysics divides into two main branches: (1) ontology (entities, their ground, essence, properties, and nature or character) and (2) formal ontology (ontological forms and categories) (Figure 9). This is a crucial distinction giving us rich resources to understand metaphysics and to do it, as we argued earlier in the context of trope theory

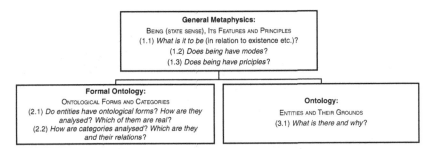

Figure 9 Main branches and basic questions of metaphysics

(see Hakkarainen & Keinänen 2016; Hakkarainen 2018). Any metaphysical problem, however specific, is informed at least implicitly by the following question formula: *what is it to be, what is there, why and in what form and category?* This formula thus unifies metaphysical questions.

Consider, for example, the following question: Is the ground of metaphysical modalities metaphysically possible worlds? If it is, are there these worlds, given some understanding of being in the state sense, its principles, features, and relation to existence and reality and so on? If there are such worlds, are these worlds abstract or concrete, on some understanding of these ontological forms or categories? Or is the ground non-modal essence? If it is, are there non-modal essences? If there are, is a non-modal essence a property or proposition, or an entity of some other category?

We suggest that this question formula is also correct about problems in different *special metaphysics* like social ontology, metaphysics of science, and ontology of mathematics. Inspired by Suárez, the distinction between general metaphysics and special metaphysics was made by the German Protestant metaphysicians in the seventeenth and eighteenth centuries, most influentially by Alexander Gottlieb Baumgarten (1714–62) (2013: 99–100) and his teacher Wolff (Darge 2014: 122; Lamanna 2014, 2021). It is still useful today although our understanding of ontology is closer to the Quineans than the conception of ontology as general metaphysics by for instance Wolff and Baumgarten. Special metaphysics are, very much like Husserl's regional or material ontologies, characterized by their different domains of the objects of investigation that are more restricted than the unrestricted domain of being in general metaphysics. Social ontology studies social entities, metaphysics of science discusses scientific objects, and ontology of mathematics investigates mathematical objects, whatever they are.[57]

---

[57] This is not intended to be an exhaustive list of possible special metaphysics. For example, Baumgarten (2013: 280) considers natural theology a special metaphysics discussing rationally

Consider for instance the problem of natural kinds in the metaphysics of science. It cannot be discussed without answering the ontological question of whether there are natural kinds, assuming something general metaphysical about being in the state sense, its features, and principles. It also needs to be specified by the ontological form of numerical distinctness: are there natural kinds numerically distinct from their members? If there are, what is their category: are they universals or particulars? If they are universals, are they kind universals or property universals? If they are particulars, are they sets or mereological sums, for instance?

This unifying question formula sets special metaphysics and ontology apart from the other fields that study what there is, such as *special sciences*. The distinctive perspective of special metaphysics and ontology to entities is that their very problem settings are informed by general metaphysics and formal ontology: general metaphysics and ontology give the *core* characteristics to special metaphysical and ontological problems. The former problems have only a more specific domain than the latter. The special scientific problems about what there is also involve general metaphysics and formal ontology, but the latter are not central when these problems are researched. It is not in the core of the problem of, say, the existence of dark matter whether being has modes.

General metaphysics and formal ontology are logically primary to special metaphysics and ontology. Regarding the relation between ontology and formal ontology, we endorse the *formal ontology first* doctrine: formal ontology is logically primary to ontology.[58] To argue that, let us consider the paradigmatic ontological problem about the existence of abstract objects such as numbers, sets, properties, and perhaps propositions. First, the very problem setting makes substantial general metaphysical suppositions: being, existence, and being real are one and the same, equally fundamental, and unitary. Here general metaphysics is logically primary to ontology. Second, the paradigmatic Quinean ontologist asks whether there are entities of a putative category or entities of an assumed ontological form, that is, abstract entities. The ontologist cannot even pose the problem without some conception of what it is to be an abstract entity. Typically, it is just assumed that abstract entities are not spatio-temporal and therefore not in causal relations and that this is Quinean *ideology* rather than ontology: 'being abstract' is just a predicate applying to certain entities rather than part of the ontological commitments (see Quine 1951). As shown in

---

the existence, being, essence, attributes, and operations of God in contrast to revealed religion. We remain neutral on natural theology as a special metaphysics.

[58] Temporal order is a distinct matter. Doing formal ontology needs not *temporally precede* the study of special metaphysical questions. Rather, they may well be studied as a part of a single process of addressing metaphysical problems.

Section 3.2, however, any answer to what it is to be an abstract entity is a substantial formal ontological assumption. Now we can see that this kind of answer is logically primary to the ontological question setting. Therefore, the answer is logically primary to any proper answer to the ontological existence question, that is, to any such ontological stance on the existence of abstract entities.

Another instance of the priority is provided by the existence of universals. We are card-carrying nominalists: we do not believe in universals. Still, we can understand what a universal would be if there were entities of such a category. We can even coherently be engaged in the formal ontological discussion on the best way of making the distinction between universals and particulars without being committed to the existence of universals (see Section 4.2.1).

However, this does not hold in the other direction when analyzing certain *putative* ontological forms and categories is concerned. Considering the formal ontological problem of what it is to be an abstract entity does not involve a specific ontological commitment to abstract entities. We may coherently ask: *if* there are abstract entities, *what is their category or ontological form analyzed by a FOR or FORs*? By contrast, the ontological question as an existence question is not hypothetical; it is whether there are *abstracta* or not. In this case, formal ontology is not on par with ontology but logically primary to it. Note that this is not an ontological commitment to the separate essence of abstractness or universality either since we do not believe in the existence of ontological forms or categories and only entities can have essences.

These results generalize because they are instances of the general nature of ontological and formal ontological problems and their relation to each other (Figure 10). As concluded earlier, ontological problems are distinctively metaphysical rather than special scientific problems. They are informed by general metaphysical and formal ontological presuppositions about being, its features, principles, forms, and categories. Formal ontology is not only logically primary but informative to the core of proper ontological study, which unifies ontological problems. Formal ontology is embedded in ontology and comes logically first. Still, in contrast to Lowe, we do not subscribe to strong essentialism about ontological forms and categories since we are not committed to the view that ontological forms and categories are grounded in the non-modal essences of entities. We do not take any stance on the a priori or posteriori status of metaphysics or any of its branch either, that is, whether the justification of metaphysical beliefs is, roughly, independent of experience or dependent on it.

Again, we can see what is fundamentally wrong with fantology, with which we started this Element. The general fantological categorial scheme of (concrete) particulars and n-adic properties (either considered as sets or sui generis entities),

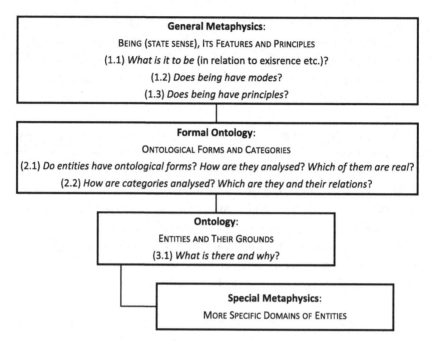

Figure 10 Branches and basic questions of metaphysics in their logical
hierarchy

still at least implicitly regulating much of ontological literature, is a theoretical
straitjacket that makes it unnecessarily difficult to formulate and defend alternative category systems or even to see their intelligibility. Those alternative systems
do not fit easily the general fantological scheme and therefore they are too easily
considered exceedingly hard to understand or even dismissed as unintelligible
although there are good grounds to take them seriously. Trope theory is one such
system. A fantological presupposition regulating metaphysical study is that
properties are property universals and/or abstract entities: universals or abstract
particulars, especially sets. But tropes are neither: they are neither universal nor
abstract.

6 Conclusion

The formal ontological approach to metaphysics, stemming from the phenomenological tradition, frees us from the fantological straitjacket and opens the
avenue for alternative views. This happens by paying serious attention to the
analysis of putative ontological forms and categories, for example, tropes and
processes, by FORs, rather than just asking the ontological existence questions.
With the assistance of the formal ontological analysis, we can properly address
ontological problems, such as whether there are tropes or processes. It provides

a useful tool for conducting ontological and metaphysical study, promoting clarity, exactness, and intelligibility, which helps us in making precise judgments about metaphysical views.

This requires a tenable meta-account of ontological forms and categories. We argued that the domain neutrality account of ontological form by Smith and Simons suffers from serious counter-examples, such as proper parthood as a FOR and processes as a category, which do not seem to be individually domain neutral regarding the domains of set theory and mathematics. Our alternative is the character neutrality account that is involved in our nominalist relationalism about ontological forms and categories, which is inspired by Lowe's and Simons' similar views.

In this Element, we have argued for our nominalist relationalism. Nominalism: ontological forms and categories are not numerically distinct entities, such as universals or sets. Relationalism: ontological forms are relational ways of existence of entities that also determine category memberships. These relational ways of existence are internal relations in the eliminativist sense: they are not entities numerically distinct from their relata. Ontological forms are not entities of any category. Rather, they are FORs in which entities stand: real relatednesses of entities. You are, for example, and your ontological form consists of the FORs actually holding of you.

Crucially, FORs are character neutral rather than domain neutral: their holding is neutral on the character of their relata (e.g., the properties of the relata). They are in principle expressible by true relational statements that do not say anything about the character of the relata without further assumptions. Formal ontological relations and hence ontological forms are character-neutral internal relations. Categories correspond then to pluralities of entities standing in the same FORs in the same order. We have shown that our metatheory of ontological forms and categories gets corroboration from the way it helps us to formulate an account of categorial fundamentality and non-fundamentality and to unify metaphysics, its questions, and branches.

References

Albertazzi, L. (2006). *Immanent Realism: An Introduction to Brentano.* Dordrecht: Springer.

Alfieri, F. (2015). *The Presence of Duns Scotus in the Thought of Edith Stein: The Question of Individuality,* trans. G. Metcalf. Dordrecht: Springer.

Aristotle (1958). *Metaphysica,* ed. W. Jaeger. Oxford: Clarendon Press.

Armstrong, D. (1978). *A Theory of Universals: Universals and Scientific Realism Volume II.* Cambridge: Cambridge University Press.

Armstrong, D. (1980). Against Ostrich Nominalism. *Pacific Philosophical Quarterly,* 61, 440–9.

Armstrong, D. (1983). *What Is a Law of Nature?* Cambridge: Cambridge University Press.

Armstrong, D. (1989). *Universals: An Opinionated Introduction.* Boulder, CO: Westview Press.

Armstrong D. (1997). *A World of States of Affairs.* Cambridge: Cambridge University Press.

Arp, R., Smith, B., & Spear, A. (2015). *Building Ontologies with Basic Formal Ontology.* Cambridge, MA: MIT Press. https://doi.org/10.2307/j.ctt17kk7vw.

Baumgarten, A. G. (2013). *Metaphysics,* trans. and ed. C. D. Fugate & J. Hymers. London: Bloomsbury.

Belt, J. (2021). Eidetic Variation: A Self-Correcting and Integrative Account. *Axiomathes,* 32, 405–34.

Bergmann, G. (1967). *Realism: A Critique of Brentano and Meinong.* Madison: The University of Wisconsin Press.

Betti, A. (2015). *Against Facts.* Cambridge, MA: MIT Press. https://doi.org/10.7551/mitpress/10139.003.0005.

Bliss, R. (2013). Viciousness and the Structure of Reality. *Philosophical Studies,* 166(2), 399–418. https://doi.org/10.1007/s11098-012-0043-0.

Brentano, F. (1973). *Psychology from an Empirical Standpoint,* trans. A. C. Rancurello, D. B. Terrell, & L. McAlister. London: Routledge.

Brentano, F. (1975). *On the Several Senses of Being in Aristotle,* trans. R. George. Berkeley: University of California Press.

Campbell, K. (1990). *Abstract Particulars.* Oxford: Blackwell.

Chrudzimski, A. (2015). Ingarden on Modes of Being. In D. Seron, S. Richard, & B. Leclercq, eds., *Objects and Pseudo-Objects: Ontological Deserts and Jungles from Brentano to Carnap.* Boston: De Gruyter, pp. 199–222.

Correia, F. (2017). Real Definitions. *Philosophical Issues*, 27(1), 52–73. https://doi.org/10.1111/phis.12091.

Correia, F., & Skiles, A. (2019). Grounding, Essence, and Identity. *Philosophy and Phenomenological Research*, 98(3), 642–70. https://doi.org/10.1111/phpr.12468.

Cumpa, J. (2011). Categoriality: Three Disputes over the Structure of the World. In J. Cumpa & E. Tegtmeier, eds., *Ontological Categories*. Heusenstamm bei Frankfurt: Ontos Verlag, pp. 15–65.

Damböck, C. (2020). (Dis-)similarities: Remarks on 'Austrian' and 'German' Philosophy in the Nineteenth Century. In D. Fisette & G. F. F. Stadler, eds., *Franz Brentano and Austrian Philosophy*. Cham: Springer, pp. 169–80.

Darge, R. (2014). Suárez on the Subject of Metaphysics. In V. M. Salas & R. L. Fastiggi, eds., *A Companion to Francisco Suárez*. Leiden: Brill, pp. 91–123.

Devitt, M. (1980). 'Ostrich Nominalism' or 'Mirage Realism'? *Pacific Philosophical Quarterly*, 61, 433–9.

Divers, J. (2002). *Possible Worlds*. London: Routledge.

Dorr, C. (2016). To Be F Is to Be G. *Philosophical Perspectives*, 30(1), 39–134. https://doi.org/10.1111/phpe.12079.

Ehring, D. (2011). *Tropes: Properties, Objects, and Mental Causation*. Oxford: Oxford University Press.

Fine, K. (1994). Essence and Modality. *Philosophical Perspectives*, 8, 1–16.

Fine, K. (1995). Ontological Dependence. *Proceedings of the Aristotelian Society*, 95, 269–90.

French, S. (2019). Identity and Individuality in Quantum Theory. In E. N. Zalta, ed., *The Stanford Encyclopedia of Philosophy* (Winter 2019 Edition). https://plato.stanford.edu/archives/win2019/entries/qt-idind/.

Giberman, D. (2021). Whole Multiple Location and Universals. *Analytic Philosophy*, 63 (4), 245-258. https://doi.org/10.1111/phib.12236.

Goodman, N., & Quine, W. V. O. (1947). Steps towards Constructive Nominalism. *The Journal of Symbolic Logic*, 12(4), 105–22.

Goris, W., & Aertsen, J. (2019). Medieval Theories of Transcendentals. In E. N. Zalta, ed., *The Stanford Encyclopedia of Philosophy* (Fall 2019 Edition). https://plato.stanford.edu/archives/fall2019/entries/transcendentals-medieval/.

Grossmann, R. (1983).*The Categorial Structure of the World*. Bloomington: Indiana University Press.

Gupta, A. (1980). *The Logic of Common Nouns*. New Haven, CT: Yale University Press.

Hakkarainen, J. (2012). Hume as a Trope Nominalist. *Canadian Journal of Philosophy*, 42(51), 55–66. https://doi.org/10.1080/00455091.2012.972129.

Hakkarainen, J. (2018). What Are Tropes Fundamentally? A Formal Ontological Account. *Acta Philosophica Fennica*, 94, 129–59. https://urn.fi/URN:NBN:fi:tuni-201909033104.

Hakkarainen, J., & Keinänen, M. (2016). Bradley's *Reductio* of Relations and Formal Ontological Relations. In H. Laiho & A. Repo, eds., *DE NATURA RERUM – Scripta in honorem professoris Olli Koistinen sexagesimum*. Turku: University of Turku, pp. 246–61.

Hakkarainen, J., & Keinänen, M. (2017). The Ontological Form of Tropes: Refuting Douglas Ehring's Main Argument against Standard Trope Nominalism. *Philosophia*, 45(2), 647–58. https://doi.org/10.1007/s11406-017-9848-6.

Hakkarainen, J., Keinänen, M., & Keskinen, A. (2018). Taxonomy of Relations. In D. Bertini & D. Migliorini, eds., *Relations: Ontology and Philosophy of Religion*. Verona: Mimesis International, pp. 93–108.

Hartimo, M. (2019). Husserl on 'Besinnung' and Formal Ontology. In F. Kjosavik & C. Serc-Hanssen, eds., *Metametaphysics and the Sciences: Historical and Philosophical Perspectives*. London: Routledge, pp. 200–15.

Hartmann, N. (2019). *Ontology: Laying the Foundations*, trans. K. Peterson. Boston: De Gruyter.

Hartung, G., King, C. G., & Rapp, C. (2019). Introduction: Contours of Aristotelian Studies in the 19th Century. In G. Hartung, C. G. King, & C. Rapp, eds., *Aristotelian Studies in 19th Century Philosophy*. Boston: De Gruyter, pp. 1–10. https://doi.org/10.1515/9783110570014-002.

Hawley, K. (2001). *How Things Persist*. Oxford: Oxford University Press.

Heil, J. (2009). Relations. In R. Le Poidevin, P. Simons, A. McGonigal, & R. P. Cameron, eds., *Routledge Companion to Metaphysics*. London: Routledge, pp. 310–21.

Heil, J. (2012). *The Universe as We Find It*. Oxford: Clarendon Press. https://doi.org/10.1093/acprof:oso/9780199596201.001.0001.

Hettche, M., & Dyck, C. (2019). Christian Wolff. In E. N. Zalta, ed., *The Stanford Encyclopedia of Philosophy* (Winter 2019 Edition). https://plato.stanford.edu/archives/win2019/entries/wolff-christian.

Hochberg, H. (2000). Facts, Truths and the Ontology of Logical Realism. *Grazer Philosophische Studien*, 58(1), 23–92.

Hochberg, H. (2013). Nominalism and Idealism. *Axiomathes*, 23, 213–34. https://doi.org/10.1007/s10516-011-9150-3.

Horsten, L. (2019). *The Metaphysics and Mathematics of Arbitrary Objects*. Cambridge: Cambridge University Press. https://doi:10.1017/9781139600293.

Husserl, E. (1969). *Formal and Transcendental Logic*, trans. D. Cairns. Dordrecht: Springer.

Husserl, E. (1970). *Logical Investigations,*trans. J. N. Findlay. London: Routledge.

Husserl, E. (1982). *Ideas Pertaining to a Pure Phenomenology and to a Phenomenological Philosophy – First Book: General Introduction to a Pure Phenomenology*, trans. F. Kersten. The Hague: Nijhoff.

Ingarden, R. (2013). *Controversy over the Existence of the World: Volume I*, trans. Arthur Szylewicz. New York: Peter Lang.

Ingarden, R. (2016). *Controversy over the Existence of the World: Volume II*, trans. Arthur Szylewicz. New York: Peter Lang.

Johansson, I. (2016). Against Fantology Again. In L. Zaibert, ed., *The Theory and Practice of Ontology*. London: Palgrave Macmillan, pp. 25–43.

Keinänen, M. (2011). Tropes – the Basic Constituents of Powerful Particulars? *Dialectica* 65(3), 419–50. https://doi.org/10.1111/j.1746-8361.2011.01276.x.

Keinänen, M., & Hakkarainen, J. (2010). Persistence of Simple Substances. *Metaphysica*, 11(2), 119–35.

Keinänen, M., Hakkarainen, J., & Keskinen, A. (2016). Why Realists Need Tropes. *Metaphysica*, 17(1), 69–85.

Keinänen, M., Keskinen, A., & Hakkarainen, J. (2019). Quantity Tropes and Internal Relations. *Erkenntnis*, 84, 519–34. https://doi.org/10.1007/s10670-017-9969-0.

Kim, J. (1993). *Supervenience and Mind: Selected Philosophical Essays*. Cambridge: Cambridge University Press.

Koslicki, K. (2012). Essence, Necessity, and Explanation. In T. E. Tahko, ed., *Contemporary Aristotelian Metaphysics*. Cambridge; Cambridge University Press, pp. 187–206.

Kotarbiński, T. (1955). The Fundamental Ideas of Pansomatism, *Mind*, 64(256), 488–500.

Lamanna, M. (2014). Ontology between Goclenius and Suárez. In L. Novák, ed., *Suárez's Metaphysics in Its Historical and Systematic Context*. Berlin: De Gruyter, pp. 135–52.

Lamanna, M. (2021). Francisco Suárez's Ontology (Science of Being). In M. Santiago de Carvalho & S. Guidi, eds., *Conimbricenses.org Encyclopedia*. www.conimbricenses.org/encyclopedia/suarez-francisco-ontology-science-of-being.

Leibniz, G. W. (1989). *Philosophical Essays*, ed. and trans. R. Ariew & D. Garber. Indianapolis: Hackett Publishing Company.

Lewis, D. K. (1983). New Work for the Theory of Universals. *Australasian Journal of Philosophy*, 61(4), 343–7.

Lewis, D. K. (1986). *On the Plurality of the Worlds*. Oxford: Basil Blackwell.

Linnebo, Ø. (2014). 'Just Is'-Statements as Generalized Identities. *Inquiry*, 57(4), 466–82. https://doi.org/10.1080/0020174X.2014.905037.

Loux, M. (1978). *Substance and Attribute*. Dordrecht: D. Reidel.

Lowe, E. J. (1998). *The Possibility of Metaphysics*. Oxford: Oxford University Press.

Lowe, E. J. (2006).*The Four-Category Ontology: A Metaphysical Foundation for Natural Science*. Oxford: Clarendon Press.

Lowe, E. J. (2009). *More Kinds of Being*. Oxford: Wiley-Blackwell.

Lowe, E. J. (2012a). A Neo-Aristotelian Substance Ontology. In T. E. Tahko, ed., *Contemporary Aristotelian Metaphysics*. Cambridge: Cambridge University Press, pp. 229–48.

Lowe, E. J. (2012b). What Is the Source of Our Knowledge of Modal Truths? *Mind*, 121(484), 919–50.

Lowe, E. J. (2013). *Forms of Thought*. Cambridge: Cambridge University Press.

Lowe, E. J. (2015). In Defence of Substantial Universals. In G. Galluzzo & M. J. Loux, eds., *The Problem of Universals in Contemporary Philosophy*. Cambridge: Cambridge University Press, pp. 65–84.

Lowe, E. J. (2018). Metaphysics as the Science of Essence. In A. Carruth, S. Gibb, & J. Heil, eds., *Ontology, Modality, and Mind*. Oxford: Oxford University Press, pp. 14–34.

MacBride, F. (2005). The Particular-Universal Distinction: A Dogma of Metaphysics? *Mind*, 114(455), 565–614.

MacBride, F. (2020). Relations. In E. N. Zalta, ed., *The Stanford Encyclopedia of Philosophy* (Winter 2020 Edition). https://plato.stanford.edu/archives/win2020/entries/relations/.

MacFarlane, J. (2017). Logical Constants. In E. N. Zalta, ed., *The Stanford Encyclopedia of Philosophy* (Winter 2017 Edition). https://plato.stanford.edu/archives/win2017/entries/logical-constants/.

Marek, J. (2021). Alexius Meinong. In E. N. Zalta, ed., *The Stanford Encyclopedia of Philosophy* (Summer 2021 Edition). https://plato.stanford.edu/archives/sum2021/entries/meinong/.

Martin, C. B. (1980). Substance Substantiated. *Australasian Journal of Philosophy*, 58(1), 3–10.

McDaniel, K. (2017). *The Fragmentation of Being*. Oxford: Oxford University Press. https://doi.org/10.1093/oso/9780198719656.001.0001.

Miller, A. (2021). Realism. In E. N. Zalta, ed., *The Stanford Encyclopedia of Philosophy* (Winter 2021 Edition). https://plato.stanford.edu/archives/win2021/entries/realism/.

Miller, J. T. (2022). Hyperintensionality and Ontological Categories. *Erkenntnis* (online first). https://doi.org/10.1007/s10670-022-00646-3.

Millière, R. (2016). Ingarden's Combinatorial Analysis of the Realism-Idealism Controversy. In S. Richard & O. Malherbe, eds., *Form(s) and Modes of Being: The Ontology of Roman Ingarden*. Bern and New York: Peter Lang, pp. 67–98.

Moran, D. (2017). Husserl and Brentano. In U. Kriegel, ed., *The Routledge Handbook of Franz Brentano and the Brentano School*. London and New York: Routledge, pp. 293–304.

Moran, D., & Cohen, J. (2012). *The Husserl Dictionary*. New York: Continuum International.

Mulligan, K. (1998). Relations: Through Thick and Thin. *Erkenntnis*, 48(2/3), 325–53.

Paul, L. A. (2017). A One Category Ontology. In J. A. Keller, ed., *Being, Freedom, and Method: Themes from van Inwagen*. Oxford: Oxford University Press, pp. 32–61.

Perovic, K. (2017). Bare Particulars Laid Bare. *Acta Analytica*, 32(3), 277–95.

Peterson, K. R. (2019). Translator's Introduction: Hartmann's Realist Ontology. In N. Hartmann, *Ontology: Laying the Foundations*. Boston: De Gruyter, pp. xv–xxxix.

Politis, V. (2004). *Routledge Philosophy Guidebook to Aristotle and the Metaphysics*. London: Routledge.

Quine, W. V. O. (1948). On What There Is. *Review of Metaphysics*, 2, 21–38.

Quine, W. V. O. (1951). Ontology and Ideology. *Philosophical Studies*, 2(1), 11–15.

Quine, W. V. O. (1953). *From a Logical Point of View*. Cambridge, MA: Harvard University Press.

Rayo, A. (2013). *The Construction of Logical Space*. Oxford: Oxford University Press. https://doi.org/10.1093/acprof:oso/9780199662623.001.0001.

Richard, S. (2015). Meinong and Early Husserl on Objects and States of Affairs. In D. Seron, S. Richard, & B. Leclercq, eds., *Objects and Pseudo-objects: Ontological Deserts and Jungles from Brentano to Carnap*. Boston: De Gruyter, pp. 123–42.

Robertson Ishii, T., & Atkins P. (2020). Essential vs. Accidental Properties. In E. N. Zalta, ed., *The Stanford Encyclopedia of Philosophy* (Winter 2020 Edition). https://plato.stanford.edu/archives/win2020/entries/essential-accidental/.

Rodriguez-Pereyra, G. (2002). *Resemblance Nominalism*. Oxford: Oxford University Press.

Rodriguez-Pereyra, G. (2017). Indiscernible Universals. *Inquiry: An Interdisciplinary Journal of Philosophy*, 60(6), 604–24.

Rodriguez-Pereyra, G. (2019). Nominalism in Metaphysics. In E. N. Zalta, ed., *The Stanford Encyclopedia of Philosophy* (Summer 2019 Edition). https://plato.stanford.edu/archives/sum2019/entries/nominalism-meta physics/.

Russell, B. (1903). *The Principles of Mathematics*. London: George Allen & Unwin.

Russell, B. (1912). *The Problems of Philosophy*. London: Williams & Norgate.

Russell, B. (1918). The Philosophy of Logical Atomism. *The Monist*, 28, 495–527.

Schaffer, J. (2009). On What Grounds What. In D. Manley, D. J. Chalmers, & R. Wasserman, eds., *Metametaphysics: New Essays on the Foundations of Ontology*. Oxford: Oxford University Press, pp. 347–83.

Schaffer, J. (2010a). The Internal Relatedness of All Things. *Mind*, 119(474), 341–76.

Schaffer, J. (2010b). Monism: The Priority of the Whole. *Philosophical Review*, 119(1), 31–76. https://doi:10.1215/00318108-2009-025.

Seibt, J. (2018). What Is a Process? Modes of Occurrence and Forms of Dynamicity in General Process Theory. In R. Stout, ed., *Process, Experience, and Action*. Oxford: Oxford University Press, pp. 120–42.

Simmons, B. (2022). Ontological Pluralism and the Generic Conception of Being. *Erkenntnis*, 87(3), 1275–93.

Simons, P. (1982). On Understanding Lesniewski. *History and Philosophy of Logic*, 3(2), 165–79.

Simons, P. (1987). *Parts: A Study in Ontology*. Oxford: Clarendon Press.

Simons, P. (1992). *Philosophy and Logic in Central Europe from Bolzano to Tarski*. Dordrecht: Kluwer Academic Publishers.

Simons, P. (1998). Metaphysical Systematics. *Erkenntnis*, 48(2/3), 377–93.

Simons, P. (2005a). Ingarden and the Ontology of Dependence. In A. Chrudzimski, ed., *Existence, Culture, and Persons: The Ontology of Roman Ingarden*. Frankfurt: Ontos, pp. 39–53.

Simons, P. (2005b). The Reach of Correspondence: Two Kinds of Categories. *Dialogue*, 44(3), 551–62.

Simons, P. (2009). Ontic Generation: Getting Everything from the Basics. In A. Hieke & H. Leitgeb, eds., *Reduction, Abstraction, Analysis. Proceedings of the 31st International Wittgenstein Symposium*. Heusenstamm bei Frankfurt: Ontos Verlag, pp. 137–52.

Simons, P. (2010). I—Peter Simons: Relations and Truth-making. *Aristotelian Society Supplementary Volume*, 84(1), 199–213. https://doi.org/10.1111/j .1467-8349.2010.00192.x.

Simons, P. (2012). Four Categories – And More. In T. E. Tahko, ed., *Contemporary Aristotelian Metaphysics*. Cambridge: Cambridge University Press, pp. 126–39.

Simons, P. (2014). Relations and Idealism: On Some Arguments of Hochberg against Trope Nominalism. *Dialectica*, 68(2), 305–15. https://doi.org/10 .1111/1746-8361.12063.

Simons, P. (2018). Lowe, the Primacy of Metaphysics, and the Basis of Category Distinctions. In A. Carruth, S. Gibb, & J. Heil, eds., *Ontology, Modality, and Mind*. Oxford: Oxford University Press, pp. 37–47.

Smith, B. (1978). An Essay in Formal Ontology. *Grazer Philosophische Studien*, 6(1), 39–62. https://doi.org/10.1163/18756735-00601004.

Smith, B. (1981). Logic, Form and Matter. *Aristotelian Society Supplementary Volume*, 55(1), 47–74. https://doi.org/10.1093/aristoteliansupp/55.1.47.

Smith, B. (1987). The Substance of Brentano's Ontology, *Topoi*, 6(1), 39–49.

Smith, B. (1989). Logic and Formal Ontology. In J. N. Mohanty & W. McKenna, eds., *Husserl's Phenomenology: A Textbook*. Lanham, MD: University Press of America, pp. 29–67.

Smith, B. (1998). Basic Concepts of Formal Ontology. In N. Guarino, ed., *Formal Ontology in Information Systems*. Amsterdam: IOS Press, pp. 19–28.

Smith, B. (2005). Against Fantology. In J. Marek & E. M. Reicher, eds., *Experience and Analysis*. Vienna: öbv&hpt, pp. 153–70.

Smith B. (2022). The Birth of Ontology. *Journal of Knowledge Structures and Systems*, 3(1), 57–66.

Smith, B., & Grenon, P. (2004). The Cornucopia of Formal-Ontological Relations. *Dialectica*, 58(3), 279–96. https://doi.org/10.1111/j.1746-8361 .2004.tb00305.x.

Smith, B., & Mulligan, K. (1983). Framework for Formal Ontology. *Topoi*, 2(1), 73–85.

Spinelli, M. (2021). Husserlian Essentialism. *Husserl Studies*, 37(2), 147–68. https://doi.org/10.1007/s10743-021-09285-y.

Stein, E. (2009).*Potency and Act: Studies toward a Philosophy of Being*, ed. L. Gelber & R. Leuven, and trans. W. Redmond. Washington, D.C.: ICS Publications.

Tahko, T. E. (2018). Fundamentality. In E. N. Zalta, ed., *The Stanford Encyclopedia of Philosophy* (Fall 2018 Edition). https://plato.stanford.edu/ archives/fall2018/entries/fundamentality/.

Tahko, T. E. (2022). Possibility Precedes Actuality. *Erkenntnis*. https://doi:10 .1007/s10670-022-00518-w.

Tahko, T. E., & E. J. Lowe (2020). Ontological Dependence. In E. N. Zalta, ed., *The Stanford Encyclopedia of Philosophy* (Fall 2020 Edition). https://plato .stanford.edu/archives/fall2020/entries/dependence-ontological.

Tegtmeier, E. (2011). Categories and Categorial Entities. In J. Cumpa & E. Tegtmeier, eds., *Ontological Categories*. Heusenstamm bei Frankfurt: Ontos Verlag, pp. 165–79.

Turner, J. (2010). Ontological Pluralism. *Journal of Philosophy*, 107(1), 5–34.

Turner, J. (2012). Logic and Ontological Pluralism. *Journal of Philosophical Logic*, 41(2), 419–48.

Vallicella, W. (2014). Existence: Two Dogmas of Analysis. In D. Novotny and L. Novak, eds., *Neo-Aristotelian Perspectives in Metaphysics*. London: Routledge, pp. 45–75.

van Inwagen, P. (2009). Being, Existence and Ontological Commitment. In D. Chalmers, D. Manley, & R. Wasserman, eds., *Metametaphysics: New Essays on the Foundations of Ontology*. Oxford: Clarendon Press, pp. 472–506.

van Inwagen, P., & Sullivan M. (2021). Metaphysics. In E. N. Zalta, ed., *The Stanford Encyclopedia of Philosophy* (Winter 2021 Edition). https://plato .stanford.edu/archives/win2021/entries/metaphysics/.

Westerhoff, J. (2005). *Ontological Categories: Their Nature and Significance*. Oxford: Oxford University Press.

Williams, D. C. (1953). On the Elements of Being I. *Review of Metaphysics*, 7, 3–18.

Williams, D. C. (1986). Universals and Existents. *Australasian Journal of Philosophy*, 64(1), 1–14.

Wilson, J. (2015). Hume's Dictum and Metaphysical Modality – Lewis's Combinatorialism. In B. Loewer & J. Schaffer, eds., *A Companion to David Lewis*. Chichester: Wiley-Blackwell.

Woleński, J. (2020). Reism. In E. N. Zalla, ed., *The Stanford Encyclopedia of Philosophy* (Winter 2020 Edition). https://plato.stanford.edu/archives/ win2020/entries/reism/.

Wolff, C. (1963). *Preliminary Discourse on Philosophy in General*, trans. R. J. Blackwell. Indianapolis: The Bobbs-Merrill Company.

Acknowledgments

We would like to thank the following people very much for questions and comments: the two anonymous referees, Jaakko Belt, Alexander Carruth, Mirja Hartimo, Rögnvaldur Ingthorsson, Anssi Korhonen, Vili Lähteenmäki, Sanna Mattila, Jaakko Reinikainen, Jenni Rytilä, Tuomas Tahko, and the students of the formal ontology seminar at Tampere University in the spring term of 2022, especially Jere Hallikainen, Maarit Heikura, Matias Moisio, Thelma Nylund, Tupuna Wäljas, and Henrik Villanen. Kone Foundation made it possible for Markku Keinänen to work on the Element. This Element is dedicated to the late E. J. Lowe (1950–2014).

Cambridge Elements

Metaphysics

Tuomas E. Tahko
University of Bristol

Tuomas E. Tahko is Professor of Metaphysics of Science at the University of Bristol, UK. Tahko specializes in contemporary analytic metaphysics, with an emphasis on methodological and epistemic issues: 'meta-metaphysics'. He also works at the interface of metaphysics and philosophy of science: 'metaphysics of science'. Tahko is the author of *Unity of Science* (Cambridge University Press, 2021, *Elements in Philosophy of Science*), *An Introduction to Metametaphysics* (Cambridge University Press, 2015) and editor of *Contemporary Aristotelian Metaphysics* (Cambridge University Press, 2012).

About the Series
This highly accessible series of Elements provides brief but comprehensive introductions to the most central topics in metaphysics. Many of the Elements also go into considerable depth, so the series will appeal to both students and academics. Some Elements bridge the gaps between metaphysics, philosophy of science, and epistemology.

Cambridge Elements ☰

Metaphysics

A full series listing is available at: www.cambridge.org/EMPH

Printed in the United States
by Baker & Taylor Publisher Services